REYES CASTILLO JR.

Starter Faith Future Leader

A Six-Week Manual for Building an Unshakable Christian Foundation

Copyright © 2025 by Reyes Castillo Jr.

All rights reserved. No part of this publication may be reproduced, stored or transmitted in any form or by any means, electronic, mechanical, photocopying, recording, scanning, or otherwise without written permission from the publisher. It is illegal to copy this book, post it to a website, or distribute it by any other means without permission.

Reyes Castillo Jr. asserts the moral right to be identified as the author of this work.

Reyes Castillo Jr. has no responsibility for the persistence or accuracy of URLs for external or third-party Internet Websites referred to in this publication and does not guarantee that any content on such Websites is, or will remain, accurate or appropriate.

Designations used by companies to distinguish their products are often claimed as trademarks. All brand names and product names used in this book and on its cover are trade names, service marks, trademarks and registered trademarks of their respective owners. The publishers and the book are not associated with any product or vendor mentioned in this book. None of the companies referenced within the book have endorsed the book.

First edition

This book was professionally typeset on Reedsy. Find out more at reedsy.com

"Before God builds your future, He strengthens your foundation. What He lays in secret becomes the strength you stand on when the world starts shaking."

— Reyes

Contents

Preface		iii
Also by Reyes Castillo Jr.		v
Letter to my readers		vii
1	Introduction	1
2	Chapter 1: Core Building Blocks for Unshakeable Faith	18
3	Chapter 2: Foundations That Change Everything	26
4	Chapter 3: Anchoring Identity: The Statement of Salvation	33
5	Chapter 4: Unlocking Obedience: Water Baptism Commitment	39
6	Chapter 5: Practicing Faith: The 21-Day Faith Log	46
7	Chapter 6: Getting Real About Faith's First Steps	53
8	Chapter 7: Realigning Your Core Foundations	61
9	Chapter 8: From Foundations to Fruit: Growing and...	68
10	Chapter 9: Real Growth Needs a Real Plan	74
11	Chapter 10: Discipleship Rhythms: The 90-Day Growth Plan	81
12	Chapter 11: Holy Spirit Activation: Prophetic and Spiritual...	87

13	Chapter 12: Living the Mission: The BLESS Evangelism...	91
14	Chapter 13: Building Real Community That Lasts	97
15	Chapter 14: Recap of Growth and Practice	104
16	Chapter 15: Keep Building; The Journey Isn't Over	110

Appendix A: The Foundation Builder's Toolkit   114
Appendix B: Lead Someone to Salvation (Simple Conversation..120
Appendix C: Scripture Declarations & Memory Cards   123
Appendix D: Foundations FAQ and Troubleshooting Guide   127

Preface

Why This Manual Exists

This book began as a response to something that kept breaking my heart.

Too many sincere believers were trying to follow Jesus with faith that wouldn't hold when life grew heavy. They loved God. They served faithfully. But when storms came, something in their foundation gave way. It wasn't because they didn't care or didn't try. It was because no one had ever shown them how to build for what lasts.

That realization changed everything for me. I had seen the same cracks in my own story, seasons where my confidence in God wavered, where ministry felt like motion without power, where prayer sounded more like survival than strength. What finally restored me wasn't a new formula or some "fresh revelation." It was going back to the basics: salvation, obedience, and daily habits that ground faith in truth instead of emotion.

Starter Faith, Future Leader was born from that rebuilding process. It isn't a collection of lessons; it's a path. One that was walked first through questions, doubt, and a longing to make faith real again. Every principle here was tested in the quiet places before it was written down.

Over the next six weeks, we will walk through the foundations that hold steady no matter the season, faith that can't be shaken because it's built on truth that doesn't move. You will find rhythms, reflection points, and real stories of people who learned to stand when life pushed hard.

This manual isn't a shortcut or a program. It's an invitation to slow down, dig deep, and build something that outlasts emotion, pressure, and time.

If your faith has felt scattered or uncertain, this is where we start again.

Not to make faith louder, but to make it stronger.

Because the Church doesn't need more impressive Christians. It needs rooted ones.

It needs believers who understand what they stand on and why.

So let's build from the beginning. Not in a rush, not for applause, but for endurance.

Let's build something that lasts.

Also by Reyes Castillo Jr.

Called by Name: Unlock the Unshakeable Identity God Already Spoke Over You

Discover the power of your God-given identity and walk in the confidence of who He already declared you to be.

The Freedom Code: The Covenant Code for Unshakable Liberty
Learn how God's covenant truth unlocks lasting freedom and delivers you from spiritual bondage.

The ELIJAH Code: Unlocking the Prophetic Gifts for End-Time Evangelism
Step into a lifestyle of prophetic purpose and bold witness in a generation that needs revival.

Finished: Living in the Power of Redemption — How the Blood of Jesus Forgives, Cleanses, and Transforms Your Life
Experience the complete work of the cross and the transforming strength of Jesus' redemption.

Seven Mantles of Fire: The Seven Dimensions of Prophetic Leadership
Uncover the spiritual mantles that equip today's leaders to

carry God's fire with integrity and power.

Letter to my readers

A Letter to My Readers

I want to start with this: thank you for showing up.

Not just for buying a book, but for choosing to dig deep when it would have been easier to stay comfortable. That choice already sets you apart more than you know.

This book is not a checklist. It is a process that will stretch you, confront you, and at times, surprise you. The truth is, growth rarely feels like victory in the moment. It feels like tension. It feels like faith being refined in real time. But that tension is where the foundation starts to harden, and that is exactly where transformation begins.

If you are anything like me, there will be days when you read a page and feel strong, and others when the words hit too close to home. Do not rush through either. Let every week do its work. The moments that sting often become the ones that save us later.

You will notice that this journey is not built around noise. It is built on steady practices such as prayer, Scripture, reflection, and community. Quiet, consistent choices that, over time, make faith unshakable. I learned that through failure, through weariness, through finding out the hard way that strength does not grow in the spotlight. It grows in surrender.

Somewhere along the way, I realized that what God builds in private always becomes someone else's lifeline in public. That is what I am praying this manual becomes for you, not just a resource, but a foundation that carries you into whatever God has next.

When the pages end, do not stop building. Keep walking. Keep showing up. Keep letting the basics shape you until they become instinct. And when someone in your life starts searching for something solid, hand them your story. Tell them what held you.

We may never meet in person, but I am praying for you, for a steady kind of faith that stands when everything else shakes. May what begins here become the start of something that does not end.

> *"Therefore, my dear brothers and sisters, stand firm. Let nothing move you. Always give yourselves fully to the work of the Lord, because you know that your labor in the Lord is not in vain."*
> — 1 Corinthians 15:58 (NIV)

With gratitude and expectation,
   Pastor Reyes

1

Introduction

People think faith is like a sturdy brick house, until a storm blows through and knocks it sideways. I watched that happen up close over the years, again and again, and honestly, it kept me awake through more than one midnight. Picture it: folks who seemed passionate, involved, showing up every week, then, wham, a crisis hits, and suddenly they're impossible to find. The faith that seemed so rock solid now scatters like dry leaves in the wind. Sometimes, I caught myself in that same drift, figuring I was immune because, well, I'd seen it all. Nobody's immune to getting knocked flat if they miss what really matters at the start.

That was my wake-up call, as real as they come. It happened during a season that, if I'm being totally transparent, almost made me pack it in. My daily pattern? Chasing answers, praying through gritted teeth, and hoping to hear from God when silence seemed to echo louder than any answer. I remember scraping myself off the floor (figuratively, mostly), opening my Bible, and feeling those old "seen it, read it, heard it" thoughts nipping at my focus every five seconds. Eventually, I got tired of staring at the ceiling wondering what I'd missed, so I decided to change how I built the foundation, for myself and for others coming behind me.

That choice wasn't just about shoring up my own belief. It was about something deeper. I remember a moment that changed everything for me. I was still early in my walk with God, hungry to grow, eager to serve. I had invited a well-known preacher. He was respected, seasoned, the kind of man people looked up to, and he came to speak at one of our events.

But as he began to teach, something didn't sit right with me. He wasn't saying anything wild or overtly heretical, but there was a subtle twist. A doctrine that clashed with what I believed in my spirit. And the worst part? I couldn't explain why.

I felt it was off. I knew it was off. But I couldn't open my Bible and prove it. I couldn't articulate my conviction in a way that brought clarity or correction.

That moment marked me. It was the day I made a personal covenant with God. I said, "Lord, I don't just want to believe. I want to know why I believe what I believe. If I'm wrong, I'm willing to be corrected. But if I'm right, I need to be rooted in truth. No more vague convictions. I want Scripture to anchor me."

From that point on, everything changed. I became a student of the Word. Not just casually reading, but digging, praying, studying, and seeking. I invested in trainings, sat under mentors, pursued sound doctrine, and cultivated a life of daily study. And now, over two decades later, I still approach the Word with the same hunger and reverence I did back then.

That moment, when I was unable to defend my faith, became the fire that forged my foundation.

And that's why foundation matters so deeply to me today.

INTRODUCTION

Because if we don't know why we believe what we believe, we won't recognize when something isn't right. And worse, we won't be able to help anyone else find the truth either.

The real test wasn't how much I could memorize, but whether my core would stand up and keep standing when job loss, family chaos, even full-on betrayal showed up at the door. Things started getting interesting. I began leaning into a few super-simple habits, nothing wild or mystical, a stretch of scripture in the morning (sometimes, right after snoozing the alarm with a groan), prayer even when my mind wandered, and, maybe the most surprising part, plugging into a prophetic community where people called out the good in me that I usually tried to hide. That combo didn't feel earth-shattering. On paper, you'd call it basic. Basic... until it worked, and I felt peace settle over my heart in ways sermons alone never quite could.

Something I never planned for was watching others take these very same rhythms and flip their entire lives around. I think of Robert, a teenager from a family that had more holes than net. No one expected much from him; even he stopped expecting anything. He started small: joining in with scripture and prayer, showing up even when he wanted to quit, grabbing hold of the idea that faith wasn't just talk but day-in, day-out stuff. One year later, he wasn't just hanging in, he was leading over a hundred teens, helping them build the same foundation that turned him from "lost cause" to anchor.

Writing *Starter Faith, Future Leader: A Six-Week Manual for Building an Unshakable Christian Foundation* came out of hundreds of true stories just like that, both messy and hopeful. This manual is for people who are ready to move beyond guessing games and borrowed faith, for those tired of hopping from one program or emotional high to another only to wind up back at the starting line. Most people don't fail because they don't care. They just haven't had the right blueprint or the right push at the right moment. We've all been handed piecemeal, scattershot approaches that leave our foundations with more gaps than cement. I decided it was time to map out something that actually sticks.

Transformation doesn't demand a secret formula hidden behind Christian jargon or some long "spiritual boot camp." You don't have to belong to a perfect family, or hit a certain "spiritual IQ," or even clean up all your loose ends to get started. Most new believers run out of steam before real change shows up. Lifelong Christians sometimes drift at the first squall. The system's been broken for a while, and religion hasn't been helping. Half the time, these old routines build more confusion than clarity.

People are tired of "sit down, be quiet, remember these rules." They want actual growth. The sticky, real kind that sticks through rough patches and comes out brighter. This book is for them. If you already think you know it all and this manual is just another filler, don't worry. Half of it was written for the know-it-alls who secretly wonder why their faith feels bland as cold oatmeal.

You can memorize doctrines, volunteer every Sunday, and even hold a mic every so often, but if the underlying patterns stay fragile, faith becomes three steps forward, four "whoops" back. You'll sense the familiar speed bumps, maybe it's apathy, or stress, or just the bland weight of daily life. These stall-outs usually happen because the basics got skipped or built on sand. Nobody brags about investing in foundations. It's invisible. But when storms shake apart what looks strong, that's when the truth jumps out. I decided to make this process so basic, so

INTRODUCTION

repeatable (and so hard for people to overcomplicate) that you can't help but see breakthrough, whether you like it or not.

This isn't a self-improvement project loaded with "just try harder" tricks. I can't stand being the guy pushing "one more thing." You'll see me poke at those old clichés and flip them over more than once. My goal is to drop all the "spiritual Olympics" and hand you something quiet, steady, and repeatable. The quickest way to kill faith is to keep moving the finish line further out. Everything inside this book follows a single thread: lay the groundwork, cement it week after week, then watch what grows up from there.

When people finally do the basics, honestly, without all the hype, they almost always start seeing God move in their lives in ways that no conference or viral social clip can substitute. This book doesn't promise easy success or a drama-free existence. If you're allergic to being challenged, this book won't help. This is for leaders (new or seasoned, willing or accidental) who want to see something permanent. They want the kind of faith that keeps building, keeps multiplying, and never gets washed away.

The book unfolds over six weeks because humans need timers. If I left it open-ended, most folks would either abandon it at week two or binge it like a TV series, only to forget everything a month later. Each week zooms in on one foundation stone, with one challenge at a time, so you can actually build muscle before you try sprinting. Expect some pushback from your "let's keep it comfortable" voice. That's normal. You'll get past it.

People worry this kind of thing will dismantle what they already have. They think if faith becomes too concrete it'll turn into rules and routines. I get it. There's a reason I spent too long in skepticism land, poking holes in systems that promised transformation but delivered cardboard spirituality. The real issue isn't routine. The "boring" blocks, laid right, are actually the only way to unlock lifelong growth. That's the surprise worth seeing. Not because it sounds good, but because it worked in dozens of lives (yes, including mine, and plenty of people who didn't want or think they needed it).

Everything inside *Starter Faith, Future Leader* moves step by step. It's a six-week trek, but one that anyone, recovering cynic or eager new believer, can get in on, together. This manual isn't the voice on stage. It's the friend in the row behind you, nudging when you stall and cheering when you grab hold. There are plenty of stories scattered throughout, for the simple reason that faith builds best when you see how grit and grace play out in real people. Every principle is paired with a rhythm, practical, small, repeatable, so that talk turns into action, and action rewires belief from the inside out.

This book came from years of meeting leaders who wanted deeper roots and stronger teams, but quietly admitted their own spiritual core felt suspect. I watched communities shrink down to a handful when the programs ended, and families quietly drift apart when nobody was bold enough to ask: what is actually being built here? That bugged me. A lot. Why spend all those Sunday mornings, all those volunteer hours, if the ground shakes once and half the garden withers?

Imagine lining up for a race with brand new sneakers, only to find out you're running on marbles instead of pavement. That's what spiritual growth feels like when the hard stuff is missing underneath. This book pours the pavement. You probably won't get a trophy at the finish line (no medals), but you will get something that keeps lasting, even on the worst days. People who push through these six weeks, the changes won't just stick, they'll multiply. And when someone else needs

INTRODUCTION

anchoring, you'll have what it takes to do more than toss out a few good-sounding "tips." You'll have the blueprint.

This isn't for pastors, super-Christians, or spiritual prodigies. Most folks who stick with this process started with questions, doubts, even some resentment that faith felt so frustrating. The only real prerequisite is being sick of shallow solutions and hungry for faith that doesn't quit.

People don't become "future leader" material by checking boxes. They become that way by choosing to fight for what lasts, over and over, even when nobody else claps. This book is your invitation into that fight. It sets up a different kind of scoreboard. Breakthroughs get measured in lives transformed, not Instagram highlights or Sunday applause. People never believe the impact that shows up after you grab hold of these basics, until they see it for themselves, usually when they're least expecting it.

Anyone ready to leave behind faith built like a house of cards, and move toward something that can hold up real families, real churches, even wild, unexpected futures, is in the right spot. *Starter Faith, Future Leader* is the tool I wish someone handed me decades ago, before life got complicated, and before I learned the slow, embarrassing way. This book is meant to save you some of the bruises, and give you the kind of anchor that can hold through anything.

You'll walk away with:

- Unpack the *Core Building Blocks for Unshakeable Faith*: why most "strong believers" crumble without them, and how to install each one so they become impossible to shake loose, even if you hit the hardest patches imaginable.
- Discover how *From Foundations to Fruit: Growing and Mul-*

tiplying Disciples* transforms dry routine into a contagious movement. People stop surviving and start multiplying the very faith that pulled them out, even beyond your circle (sometimes way past your comfort zone).
- Dive into the raw process of *Establishing Salvation, Baptism, and Faith as the Initial Pillars*. Not as decorations or handy labels, but as the starting place for every breakthrough, releasing strength that nobody can steal, not even on your worst day.
- Watch the power of *Discipleship, Holy Spirit Empowerment, and Evangelism in Action* flip bland duty into unstoppable passion. You become the kind of leader who doesn't burn out but raises up others, again and again, no matter how "ordinary" you feel right now.

The difference isn't in the information. It's in the rhythms, the way you live them out, and how each one keeps paving the way for the next. Skipping a step leads to circling right back here. Do it right the first go.

Throughout the chapters ahead, you'll hit points where your brain throws up the "this is too simple" warning flags. That's your comfort zone panicking. Ignore it. Simple means doable, which means this time you won't just talk about transformation. You'll experience it in ways that last longer than the current hype cycle.

Quick disclaimers: you'll see sarcasm, a decent helping of humility (took a lot to get here), and maybe a sideways jab at overcomplicated spirituality. Life's tough enough without church jargon weighing down the backpack. You'll get stories, challenges, and reflection points. You'll also get the permission to start where you're at (baggage included, no extra charge),

INTRODUCTION

and keep going even when all you have is a tiny spark left.

The change you're about to see doesn't just show up in your faith notes or journal. It'll outlast busy seasons, drama, disappointment, and every curveball you didn't sign up for. The only thing you have to lose is whatever's been keeping you stuck.

Time to set the first stone in place. One block, one real-life story, and one group rhythm at a time.

About the author

Some people look at faith as if it's some kind of invisible shield, one that keeps every storm at bay. You know... the idea that, if you just have enough belief, confusion won't creep in, and rough times stay far away? I never had that luxury. To be honest, I doubt anyone can claim they truly do.

Let's start here. I've spent more years walking alongside uncertain Christians than counting the miles from my door to the church. These years, over twenty actually, if you're the counting type, brought front-row seats to stories where folks set out eager, hearts on fire, only to freeze up once life delivered a punch that didn't follow the "how-to" handouts. That was always the pattern. People imagined, maybe you have too, that once you "really got saved," or you checked baptism off your list, you'd be steel. Then the wind picked up, relationships got rocky, a diagnosis or a job loss landed... and just like that, what seemed solid yesterday felt slippery.

This isn't just noise from the pulpit or a cautionary tale for the youth group. I watched, absolutely helpless at first, as one family I'd poured my guts into completely unraveled when their oldest got sick. Faith, Bible knowledge, community... they had those things, or at least the outlines. But none of it "held" under the pressure. Maybe you think that's unusual. I'll say this. After the fifth or sixth similar experience in a row, you stop brushing it off as bad luck or blaming culture. The real issue won't leave you alone. I had to ask: what are we missing? What's the missing piece that keeps these good people from standing their ground when the bottom drops out?

So I got stubborn about it. I watched, took notes, then started a weird habit. Late nights reading old books, journals, sermon transcripts. Sometimes I'd pray in the dark, pacing my kitchen, asking God for an answer that made sense. Most of the time, nobody saw the turmoil. They only saw my Sunday smile. They didn't know about the questions that kept echoing back at me after the last handshake in the foyer. There's a myth, I guess, that pastors have answers lined up like soup cans in a pantry. Always ready to grab the one you need. I wanted that to be true. It's not.

Other times, frustration would push me to experiment, anything to break the pattern. If a usual study guide left people yawning, I'd scrap it and hunt for some way... any way... to get real traction. At first, what happened didn't look impressive on the outside. We'd try tighter small groups. Sometimes they fizzled. I tried direct mentoring. Results sometimes, but too much depended on personalities and, honestly, chemistry between folks. With each try, something small stuck, but nothing felt like a breakthrough. It bugged me. People shouldn't have to fail six times before piecing together a faith that actually "holds."

Over time, I spotted a thread. Whenever folks grabbed hold of some real, gritty truth about salvation, not the Sunday School version, but the kind that won't let you off easy, they changed. Not everyone, and not instantly, but enough that I started paying closer attention. They'd lose less time second-guessing

INTRODUCTION

themselves when storms hit. They'd stick through confusion, fight less with guilt, and tap into a stubborn hope that felt... how can I say it... more like bedrock than wishful thinking.

These weren't just rare success stories. They were the result of something repeatable. Each time someone stuck with it, practiced the basics, learned how to keep showing up (even when the old habits screamed for their attention), the outcome became less random. This wasn't magic. It was slow, imperfect, painfully human growth. Yet it outlasted the quick fixes, self-help trends, even the "spiritual shortcuts" that never really paid off.

My own process, by the way, didn't come insulated from embarrassment. More than once, I missed the signs. I'd push a program or a study series, only to watch it unravel in the real world. I knew the feeling of preparing, praying, believing it would "work." Then realizing that real discipleship, the kind that sticks, isn't built by hoping hard enough. It's forged in habits, honest accountability, and a willingness to start small. Kind of a letdown if you're after a flashy breakthrough story. But true.

Let's talk about failure for a second. I've dropped the ball... sometimes pretty badly... on things that seemed obvious in hindsight. I can recall one young guy who showed up, all questions and nervous energy, desperate for answers I thought were simple. I rattled off my usual encouragements, gave him the right verses, and watched him vanish a month later. Another family, a sweet one, if you're asking, signed up for everything. But when trouble crashed in, they scattered. It stings. Each time, I'd think: what on earth am I missing?

Eventually, after a lot of dead ends, I landed on something basic, but overlooked. The foundation matters more than the window dressings. I stopped assuming folks "got" the essentials just because they sat through the membership class or recited the expected answers in a group. I got a bit relentless about drilling deep on salvation. What it is, what it isn't, what it actually changes inside a person. Then I'd nudge people to wrestle with baptism, not just as a tradition or checkmark, but as an act of real, lived commitment. When the basics took root, the rest started lining up. Often slowly, sometimes with setbacks, but growing anyway.

Of course, discovering this wasn't just a personal win. It changed how I approached everything else. Leadership, teaching, even the way I listened during tough counseling sessions. These programs and curricula stacked up lessons about "going deeper" or "living victoriously," but skipped the groundwork. That's why people, good ones, kept scattering and stalling out when the pressure hit. They didn't lack passion or interest. They just didn't have a clear, grounded place to stand when things went sideways.

I got tired of patching things up after the fact. I wanted a way for folks to get anchored before the storm showed up. Something you could really call a foundation, not just another set of catchy slogans or quick wins.

The years that followed, full of experiments, do-overs, unexpected surprises, taught me to build slower, but build for real. Accountability became a big deal. So did habits, small, repeatable actions, not glamorous on their own, but powerful in the long haul. Prayer stopped being a "spiritual extra" and started showing up as my lifeline, especially when exhaustion set in.

If you're picturing all this as one never-ending spiritual boot camp, you're missing the point. There were easy days, hard

INTRODUCTION

days, some weeks where nobody showed up and I considered quitting. Other times, a simple, honest conversation did more than any hundred-page workbook. I don't have a secret stash of superpowers. Lots of coffee, sure, but nothing more impressive than persistence and a belief that God is more patient than I am.

That brings us to why Starter Faith, Future Leader even exists. It grew because I was tired of watching scattered efforts lead to scattered people. The usual patchwork approach, grab one book about faith, another about spiritual gifts, then a lesson or two on evangelism, hope the loose ends tie up somewhere, never really equipped anyone for the tough stretches. I wanted something different. Something you could actually use, day by day, week after week.

People needed clarity. A guide that didn't assume too much, didn't skip ahead, and wouldn't let foundational cracks go unchecked.

So, I set out to build this manual for people like the ones I sat with. Over coffee, in parking lots, at hospital bedsides, when they said, "I want to be ready next time life gets hard, but I don't know where to start." Through each draft, I kept circling back to the same truths: anchored salvation, visible obedience, habits that outlast mood swings, gifts that actually get used, and a faith that can't be shaken when storms roll through.

Some might wonder if it really works. After years of watching good people drop out or burn out, skepticism is fair. But over time, I saw timid, unsure folks, some barely hanging on, grow into leaders who wouldn't flinch even when opposition hit. That's what happens when the foundation is solid and the basics don't get skipped. These are men and women who no longer see faith as window dressing, but as the core of every decision, every action, every response when things get messy.

Quick fixes or "one-size-fits-all" magic don't help. My process is a grind. Sometimes slow, sometimes awkward, always involving real life. Yet I've seen the transformation that's possible when everyday Christians stop chasing spiritual fads and dig deep into what actually lasts.

Before all this, many leaders felt unsure, scattered, and a little powerless. They'd drift from one program to another, always hoping the next one would "stick." That cycle just wears people out. But now, after embracing a sturdier, step-by-step manual, I see leaders who walk with conviction. Who don't hang back when things get tough. Who lead their families and groups with a confidence that doesn't need to shout to be real.

The goal isn't to build "successful" Christians. I want a generation of believers too stubborn to quit when life gets ugly. People who have worked through the tough questions, studied, messed up, and got back up. The kind whose joy isn't held together by circumstances, but by truth that's sharp enough to stand up to hardship.

My passion for this really boils down to multiplication. Passing on a steady, joy-filled faith that can weather anything. Not by handing out more rules, but by sharing the tools I found through years of trial, error, and some honest suffering. Multiplying grounded disciples isn't about making clones. It's about launching people who'll pass on the same foundation, but who'll do it in their own skin, in their own families and neighborhoods.

My life as a pastor hasn't been all victory laps and highlight reels. When things got ugly, and my own faith took a few knocks, it was always accountability, real, honest friends who asked hard questions, that kept me from drifting away. There's no substitute for that. Each rough patch ended up driving me deeper into Scripture. Sometimes with more confusion than clarity, but always with a little more grit.

Some folks ask if I ever considered quitting. More times than I'll admit. Each new round of discouragement seemed to come with its own flavor. Ministry politics, burnout, spiritual dryness. Every time, though, God used those cycles to sand off some pride and sharpen my focus. I learned pretty late that long-term fruit comes from a long obedience. There's no trick to it. Just a steady drip of small choices over time.

At one point, I actually tried stepping away and letting others carry the load, shrinking my circle so failure wouldn't sting as much. It didn't work. You can't sidestep your calling for long without a gnawing sense that something's missing. I drifted right back into the mess because, even on my worst days, I can't ignore the reality that people are starving for truth that holds. Can't unsee what I've seen.

"Equipping leaders for generational impact" means sticking with people through their highs and lows. Refusing to let temporary setbacks define their future. Fighting for the kind of legacy that leaves their kids and grandkids grounded. Not in my name, but in the kind of faith that's bigger than programs or personalities.

All those years, twenty-plus now, taught me to love the slow, patient work of building people up from square one. It's not dramatic. Nobody gives you medals for consistency. Most days, you feel like you're just repeating yourself. Yet, when you look back, you realize those "little" moments, one-on-one talks, prayers whispered over the phone, awkward silences in a counseling room, are where the deepest work happens. The "secret" to lasting transformation isn't really a secret. It's just persistence, willingness to get your hands dirty, and a refusal to let people walk away from grace.

This manual isn't a polished, pain-free path. What's on offer is a clear, structured way forward. But it's one that requires honesty, humility, and a stubborn refusal to settle for surface-level faith. I designed every piece of this manual with the scattered, the doubting, the "I should know better but don't" crowd in mind. Because that's what I needed, too.

Once people get grounded, really deeply planted, they stop scattering when storms hit. Instead, they find themselves holding steady, even when everyone else seems to be ducking for cover. It doesn't always look heroic. A lot of the time, it just looks like showing up, doing the next right thing, and refusing to hide. But that's how leaders are born. The kind who last.

This book exists because scattered programs and curriculum left people wandering. I wanted to hand off something better. Something tested in real messes. Something you can actually use. More than that, I wanted to help you sidestep the mistakes that took me years to realize, so you can dig in with confidence.

The people I admire most, the ones who stick it out even when applause fades, never got there by accident. They built a foundation brick by brick, lesson by hard-won lesson. They didn't have secret knowledge. They just decided to go deep on the basics, over and over. It's not glamorous. It's rarely quick. It works.

This isn't about me or even about teaching. What matters is the transmission, the actual passing along of a faith that sticks. A joy that can't be shaken when things turn upside down. If you've struggled through programs that fizzle, or if you've ever felt yourself stalling, you're in good company. I've been there. Most people have.

It doesn't have to stay that way. With clear steps, honest

effort, and a refusal to let discouragement win, you can build a life that holds. And that's exactly what Starter Faith, Future Leader: A Six-Week Manual for Building an Unshakable Christian Foundation was built to help you do.

2

Chapter 1: Core Building Blocks for Unshakeable Faith

"A foundation is the unseen yet essential element of any structure. Without a firm foundation, no lasting building can stand."
– Rick Warren, *The Purpose Driven Life*

You know the feeling when you walk into an old, beautiful house? There's that strange confidence, like you're standing on something that's survived storms, time, all kinds of drama...and yet, it doesn't shout about its strength. The floors might creak, the doors might stick, but underneath, there's something solid that holds everything steady. The real security is hidden. You never see the foundation. Still, it's the only reason the place makes it through wind, rain, or wild holiday parties.

When I started wrestling with faith, I wanted that kind of bedrock. I'd seen a lot of people drift. Their beliefs sometimes changed depending on who they dated or what podcast got stuck in their heads that week. I didn't want to be one of those folks who fumble around, never really sure where they stand, bouncing from one spiritual trend to the next. Eventually, everyone gets tired of wandering. My focus turned to figuring

CHAPTER 1: CORE BUILDING BLOCKS FOR UNSHAKEABLE FAITH

out what actually gives a faith that outlasts all the ups and downs. It's not some mystical secret, and it's not reserved for people with perfect pedigrees. The strongest faith starts with three basic building blocks: knowing you're saved (for real), stepping into baptism like you mean it, and understanding exactly what it means to trust.

Clarity didn't drop into my lap one morning. Nobody just wakes up and says, "I'm secure forever, nothing can shake me." There's some elbow grease involved, sometimes a good bit of doubt too. Maybe you'll recognize part of your own story in these first steps. The whole idea of salvation can sound like churchy jargon at first. Same goes for baptism. It's easy to assume it's just a symbolic bath, a one-time appearance in front of family, or that thing churches schedule between Sunday school and potluck. Faith has picked up a pile of buzzwords over the centuries, and sometimes they sound like white noise. But once you dig in, these ideas turn out to matter more than expected. When you figure out what's at stake, you want firm answers.

This chapter isn't about memorizing the "correct" answers for some heavenly pop quiz. Nobody's handing out gold stars for perfect doctrine recitation. This is about anchoring yourself to something that doesn't wash away when life gets unpredictable, inconvenient, chaotic, and occasionally hilarious in the worst timing possible. If you've replayed old mistakes or second-guessed whether you really belong, you're not crazy. You're not alone. Everyone I trust has had some version of that internal wrestling match. There's something in us that wants the clarity to say, "Yeah, no matter what comes, I actually know where I stand."

Why Start With the Basics? Because Pretending Gets Ex-

hausting

There's nothing more exhausting than pretending you know what you believe, only to get blindsided by life and realize you were just parroting someone else's script. A quick story: years ago, I watched a friend, smart, thoughtful, raised going to church, hit a rough patch. Trouble at work. Health issues in the family. The works. All those Bible verses and songs he'd memorized as a kid seemed to evaporate under pressure. He told me, "It's like everything I thought I believed just slipped through my fingers. I don't even know if it was ever real." That shook me. Deep down, I knew I could end up in the same boat if I didn't have something more than Sunday school answers.

This is why I keep dragging the spotlight back to the foundation. It's not glamorous. Nobody throws a party for "basic salvation understanding" or "clarity on baptism." Balloons and confetti aren't required for something to be vital. I don't care about impressing the crowd. I care about standing steady when the crowd disappears or turns hostile. The older I get, the more allergic I am to religious performance. Faith built for the spotlight falls apart when you're alone and scared. I want the kind of faith that can survive a storm, a scandal, or even my own self-sabotage.

Anchoring Your Identity, Why "Salvation" Isn't A Buzzword

Salvation gets tossed around so much it starts to lose shape. At its core it's about identity. Are you really safe, really wanted, or just on trial all the time? People define themselves with jobs, hobbies, relationships, even "good vibes." That works until something goes sideways. Lose a job, go through a breakup, or one rough month...and suddenly there's nothing that sticks. I've chased after every label, thinking, "Maybe this next thing

CHAPTER 1: CORE BUILDING BLOCKS FOR UNSHAKEABLE FAITH

will prove I'm worth something." Then it doesn't.

Looking closely at what it means to be rescued and claimed shifted the whole conversation in my mind. Instead of scrambling for constant reassurance, you tap into something steady: "I'm not defined by my failures, or even my highs. I'm anchored in a promise." Imagine waking up with the certainty that you're not earning your place on some invisible scoreboard. No more bargaining. No more pretending you've got it all together. Just the solid fact: you belong, not because you performed, but because you were invited and said yes. Relief doesn't even begin to cover it. I did try to find loopholes or reasons it shouldn't count for me. Old habits.

Many people aren't as secure as they look. There's a scramble for identity underneath. A foundation that tells you where you stand isn't just helpful. It's game-changing. That's why we start here: every other part of faith builds on getting this question settled.

Baptism, Why Jumping In Isn't Optional

If your experience with baptism is awkward family photos and a quick dunk in lukewarm water, you might wonder why this step gets so much attention. I once tried to talk myself into skipping baptism entirely. "It's just a symbol," I said. "Isn't it the heart that counts?" True, but sometimes the heart needs a nudge and a public moment to mark the shift from old to new. I know people who agonized for months, waiting to feel "ready." Others just did it because everyone else was, then never thought about it again. Both miss the point. It's not about perfection or performance. Baptism says, "I'm done living like I belong to myself." It's that line in the sand. Cross it, and you can't claim ignorance or pretend you're just "checking it out" anymore.

When I finally took the plunge, something clicked. The doubts and hesitations didn't vanish, but a new kind of clarity showed up. A shift happens when you say something publicly. When you let your old labels wash off and step into a new reality. It's concrete, even if it happens in front of soggy friends and relatives. For me, the moment was, "Okay, I can't go backward. I'm all in." It was both thrilling and terrifying. If you don't feel a little exposed, you might be sleepwalking through it.

Baptism isn't just a ritual. It's one of those rare moments where you say, "This is who I am now." The world may not throw a parade, but your internal compass locks onto something that resists getting knocked off course every Monday morning.

The "Faith" Part, Knowing and Trusting Are Not the Same

People sometimes talk about faith as if it's wishful thinking or pretending problems don't exist. I used to fall into that trap. Keep it vague, keep it safe. Actual faith isn't about ignoring reality. It's about staking your life on something you're convinced is true, even when your feelings are all over the place. There's a difference between knowing facts about something and trusting it enough to lean your whole weight on it.

Plenty of folks can quote verses about grace, love, and eternal security, then live like they're still auditioning for approval. I did that for a long time. Faith flips the switch from "maybe, hopefully, someday" to "right now, it counts for me." It's not a leap into darkness. It's a step onto what's already been promised. The bravest people aren't the ones who never doubt. They move forward in spite of it, again and again, until trust becomes muscle memory.

Faith is more durable than hype. Motivation runs out. Feelings fluctuate. Spiritual trends change. Knowing who you trust, and why, becomes a stabilizer when everything else gets wobbly.

Settling In (But Not Settling Down)

CHAPTER 1: CORE BUILDING BLOCKS FOR UNSHAKEABLE FAITH

Once you've grabbed onto salvation, baptism, and faith, it's tempting to think you're done building. Not even close. The best structures don't just rely on the initial concrete pour. They get regular checkups. Small cracks get filled. Foundations get reinforced as new floors get added. That's where real growth starts. This chapter isn't about getting the right answers and coasting. It's permission to finally stop circling the "Am I really in?" question and step into something solid so you can move forward. Think about how much energy you've spent in spiritual limbo just trying to keep up appearances.

When your identity is settled, you stop scrambling for validation. When baptism marks the line, you've got a reference point that doesn't shift. When faith becomes trust, not just theory, you start to relax, even laugh at your own second-guessing. That frees up mental bandwidth for everything else life throws at you.

This isn't hype. It's the benefit of having a foundation that actually holds, whether anybody notices or not. You don't have to manufacture certainty. You can rest in it, even if it's quiet and there's no applause. If your head's spinning from all the talk about basics and steady ground, that's fine. Stick around. This is only the groundwork. The real adventure builds from here.

What Happens When You Actually Get Grounded

"Being grounded" isn't mysterious. It means you don't panic when circumstances change. You recognize your value isn't tied to your latest failure or success. There's an inner confidence, an "I know who I am," that shows up quietly: in conversations, in how you respond to criticism, or when life doesn't go your way. Anchoring your identity in something unchanging isn't restrictive. It's liberating. You let go of the exhausting project of self-invention. You can be honest. You can admit when you have no answers.

Clarity and security in salvation don't make you arrogant. They make you less defensive and more open. You spend less time protecting your image and more time growing, trying, and learning. Once you've got this foundation, the risks that once scared you seem smaller. The questions that used to keep you up at night start to lose their edge. You're not immune to doubt, but you are immune to despair.

I think about my younger self, constantly searching for shortcuts or new angles. The old, plain building blocks, salvation, baptism, faith, do more heavy lifting than any flashy "advanced" techniques I once thought I needed. If you want a faith that grows and outlasts tough seasons, you can't skip these first steps. There's no way around it. That's good news. Nobody's keeping this out of your reach.

You Never Graduate From the Foundation

After all this talk about beginnings, the reality is you never graduate from them. Every time life throws a curveball, I circle back to the basics. That's not failure. That's how strong things stay strong. No skyscraper ever says, "I don't need my basement anymore." The security and clarity from these starting points become the scaffolding for every new step, every challenge, every chance to grow.

If you're feeling restless or impatient, wanting to skip to "deeper" things, don't sell the basics short. They'll carry you farther than expected. The most unshakeable faith isn't built on secrets, shortcuts, or elite knowledge. It's built on these first, stubborn building blocks. Put them in place, and you're set up not just to survive, but to thrive, through storms, seasons, and surprises.

Ready? Let's see how firm this thing can get. You might discover you're already standing on more solid ground than you think. And it's only just getting started.

3

Chapter 2: Foundations That Change Everything

The Starting Point Most People Miss

Let's get something straight, so many folks stumble right out of the gate. Not because they're lazy or stubborn, but because somewhere along the line, they've picked up the idea that spiritual life is private. You hear it all the time, "I said the prayer, that's good enough," or, "Faith is something that grows on its own, right?" If that's been your thinking, you're definitely not alone. These early steps, salvation, baptism, and daily faith, aren't suggestions or advanced moves for spiritual "overachievers." They're the very first building blocks. Miss these, and everything else gets wobbly fast.

People love to point out that God looks at the heart. Absolutely true. But scripture doesn't stop there. Romans writes about confessing with your mouth. Something different happens when faith goes public, when you stop keeping it a secret and instead declare, out loud, your whole new identity.

Leaders sometimes overcomplicate this or avoid talking about it for fear of making newcomers feel awkward. The first followers didn't do that. In Acts, Peter got right to the point: believe, get baptized, and start living it out right away. No waiting periods. That pattern still works today.

What Changes When Foundations Are Set

There's a weird sense of relief and certainty that pops up when you finally know where you stand. Ask anyone who's ever taken these steps for real. There's nothing quite like moving from "I hope I'm saved" to "I know where my life is rooted." This isn't about feeling something emotionally charged every minute. Feelings are unpredictable. When you anchor yourself in clear steps, actual steps, not fuzzy intentions, confidence starts sneaking in.

Matthew talks about lives built on a rock. That image sounds nice. It means if you've actually done what Jesus said, not just thought about it or half-heartedly copied what your parents did, you're ready for whatever life throws at you. Early Christians proved this wasn't just a theory. Those who started with the apostles' teaching, public confession, immediate baptism, daily faith, stuck it out.

Skip this, and the cracks show up. Maybe not today, probably not tomorrow, but eventually, something shakes your world and the old uncertainty returns. I've walked alongside people who spent years feeling unsure, always circling back to the basics. The fix is to go back to the start. Do what the first believers did, in the same order.

Salvation: Not a Magic Spell, But a Real Reset

You hear stories about dramatic conversions. Some folks worry theirs wasn't emotional or exciting enough. That's not what matters. At its core, salvation means trusting that Jesus did what you couldn't and then actually telling somebody, out loud, on purpose. The "confess with your mouth" part is stressed for a reason. You're declaring a transfer, a new citizenship, a total shift in status. It's not just a mental "yes" or a quiet feeling inside.

People often ask if quietly saying a prayer is enough. Faith in scripture is both internal and external. If your new life doesn't quite feel "new," check if you ever went public with it. I've met many people who felt stuck until they put words to what God had done. That step out of the shadows does something inside you. Suddenly, you're not worried about losing it or doing it wrong.

Leaders need to make this step unmissable. Walk through it clearly. Let people declare it. Don't just give them a handout or a private form. You're handing them a new identity.

Baptism: The No-Drama, No-Delay Command

Next up: baptism. It isn't a "when you get around to it" sort of thing. The earliest believers didn't treat it like an optional upgrade. When someone believed, baptism happened almost right away. It's the first step of obedience. A public statement. A line in the sand. It's a way for people to say, "I'm in, and I'm not turning back."

Some say baptism isn't urgent or that it's just a symbol. That's one way to avoid it. Acts 2:38 shows baptism as part of the natural response to faith. I've watched many people walk in circles spiritually, hoping for momentum or clarity, but never quite getting there. When they stopped treating baptism as a "someday" thing, everything changed.

Some leaders are nervous about pushing baptism too soon. They worry about rushing people. When people delay, their doubts multiply. When they act quickly, doubts lose their grip. Identity sticks, and they move forward. I've seen some of the most directionless folks find traction the moment they commit publicly.

It doesn't need to be complicated. No need for a perfectly planned event or a huge crowd. What matters is stepping forward, publicly, in obedience. The details of who's watching or how polished the ceremony looks change nothing about what's happening at a heart level.

Faith: The Everyday Grind (and Why That's a Good Thing)

Now, faith. Many people treat it like a light switch, you flip it at salvation, and the rest takes care of itself. The stories I remember, the ones that stuck, were about people who didn't expect faith to grow on autopilot. The real change happens in daily routines. Seeing God at work, even when you're not really feeling it that day.

Paul writes in Colossians about continuing to live in Christ. "Continue" isn't passive. It asks for deliberate steps, practicing trust, testing obedience, noticing small ways God shows up. The people with the deepest faith often have stories of struggle, confusion, or lost hope. Faith toughens up in the middle of daily friction.

Leaders who help people build daily habits, prayer, reading, honest reflection, help faith fill in the cracks. It's not about catching a feeling. It's about showing up again and again. Momentum builds. Confidence grows. Crisis faith becomes durable faith.

Some say faith just grows naturally. That might happen in small ways. But I've met dozens who waited, hoping faith would just grow. The result was frustration and doubt. Some gave up entirely. Those who made a pattern, intentional action, honest prayers, simple obedience, found that faith showed up when needed.

Why People Mess This Up (And What Actually Works)

Some classic mistakes come up over and over. First, the feelings trap. If you wait to feel ready, confident, or worthy, you'll wait a long time. Salvation doesn't depend on your mood. Baptism isn't a reward for feeling spiritual. Faith doesn't appear only after doubt is gone. These steps are rooted in what Christ already did, not in how you feel about it on Tuesday afternoon.

Another mistake is delaying baptism. Leaders sometimes say, "Let's give it time." That delay creates insecurity and doubt. Baptism severs the old way of life. It's a final break from half-in, half-out living. If you want traction, obey quickly.

Finally, brushing off daily steps of faith. Growth that lasts always has a routine. No one stumbles into maturity. You build it, slowly, intentionally, with daily moves. Miss this, and you'll always wonder if you're really growing at all.

If any of this sounds familiar, the fix is clear. Anchor your assurance in Christ's work. Step out in public obedience. Practice faith daily until it reshapes how you see and respond to everything.

Pushback and How It Usually Fails

Some objections come up a lot. "I already said the prayer. Isn't that enough?" Or, "Baptism just isn't that important right now, shouldn't I wait until it feels right?" Or, "Faith will develop when the time's right."

These objections make sense from a certain angle. Scripture doesn't support them. Romans makes faith public. Acts shows baptism as immediate. Long-term faith stories always start with intentional steps, not accidental growth.

If you want to keep wondering, treat these as optional. If you're tired of guessing, root yourself in what's clear, public, and proven to last. Simple steps are effective steps.

Proof That This Works, For Anyone

CHAPTER 2: FOUNDATIONS THAT CHANGE EVERYTHING

This worked for early believers who faced incredible pressure. They didn't just have private hope. Their practices made them stand out, even when Rome opposed them.

It's still happening. I've met people from chaotic backgrounds who found stability after taking clear steps: declaring faith, getting baptized, practicing small daily acts. Not overnight, but steadily.

Robert's story fits here. He spent years feeling like he was never truly "in." Always doubting. The day he said yes to baptism, weeks after finding assurance, that's when things turned. He found traction. Faith had roots.

How to Actually Guide New Believers (and Why It Matters)

If you're leading others, the job is clear. Don't bury new believers in theology. Don't overwhelm them with rules. Give them three things: clarity about salvation, opportunity for immediate baptism, and simple routines to practice faith.

Walk with them. Don't just toss instructions their way. Help them tell the truth about who they are now. Support their step into baptism. Encourage daily trust, even when it feels small. These steps build momentum. Get them wrong, and you're fixing things that should've been built right from the start.

When leaders return to this model, change happens. New believers stop second-guessing. Old doubts vanish. Real transformation shows up, not just in how people talk, but how they live. Whole communities shift by returning to the basics. No need for fancy methods. Just the simple, public, daily actions the earliest followers took for granted.

Wrapping Up (Without Actually Wrapping Up)

The foundations for a vibrant spiritual life aren't up for debate. Salvation is declared with your mouth. Baptism is done quickly, in public. Faith is practiced every day in real ways. There's room for questions. Eventually, you move forward because you trust God's process more than your own ideas.

If confusion or delay has been your pattern, now's a good time to stop it. Circle back to these basics. Start here. You won't regret it, and neither will the people you're guiding.

4

Chapter 3: Anchoring Identity: The Statement of Salvation

So let's just be real from the jump, believing something one day and doubting it the next can get exhausting. If you're anything like most people who start out wanting to follow Jesus, there's a good chance you've felt rock solid about your faith one morning, then, by lunch, you're second-guessing your own heart. I've been there. The struggle is anything but rare. I've watched it in others, and honestly, I've lived it myself. The question that simmers underneath is simple but stubborn: How do I actually know what's real when my feelings are playing ping-pong with my confidence?

Most folks don't talk about it, but the numbers don't lie, almost 40% of young Christians today wonder about their salvation. Some people pretend they're made of stone, but even the most stoic get rattled when the inner weather changes. Billy Graham, who made his living helping people get clear about faith, said you can't build a stable spiritual life on raw emotion. He's not wrong. Our feelings flip like a cheap diner pancake. Truth, on the other hand, doesn't budge. Anchoring yourself to something that stands up when everything else crumbles is essential.

Why Your Identity Feels Like Quick Sand (And Why That's Totally Normal)

Faith isn't a magic pill for insecurity. People often expect a steady high, then get thrown if a shadow of doubt creeps in. Half the time, we're not doubting actual facts, we're reacting to bad moods, stress, or being tired. You spill coffee on your shirt, you fail a test, or your boss snaps at you, and suddenly your brain decides maybe you're not worth much. Doubts flare up in those moments because emotions are terrible fact-checkers.

To move from that shaky ground onto something that doesn't tremble every time life takes a detour, you need a new anchor. Building your core sense of who you are on something bullet-proof and enduring replaces the emotional yo-yo. That's where the Statement of Salvation comes in.

The Statement of Salvation: Putting Truth on Paper (And in Your Face)

Grab a pen, open a blank page, and write out, in your own words, your Statement of Salvation. Don't overthink it. This is not about impressing seminary professors. It's about clarifying, once and for all, what Jesus did, how you've responded, and what that makes you, right now.

The basics:

1. What did Jesus actually do?
2. How have you personally responded?
3. Who are you now because of it?

Some people use specific verses, Romans 8:16 is a favorite: God's Spirit confirms that you're God's child. Use it if you want, or stick to your story. Writing it out forces you to nail down fuzzy ideas and call out the truth in black and white.

Once that's done, sign and date your page. Treat it as you would any important contract. Your signature is a line in the sand: "This is who I am. This is settled."

Seven Days of Reading: Why Repetition Isn't Just for Kids

Read your statement out loud every morning for one week. There's a reason for this. When you declare something true about yourself out loud, your brain starts to treat it as more real.

This step retrains how your brain responds when emotional doubts try to sneak back in. You're taking the steering wheel and deciding that mood won't call the shots anymore. This is not just positive thinking. It's aligning your sense of self with something done outside of you, not just what's happening inside today.

Getting Real: Daily Check-Ins Without the Fake Smiles

Each day, after you read your statement, message or chat with someone who's walking alongside you. If you're leading a group, reach out, ask how it's going, and actually listen. Avoid defaulting to "everything's fine" if it's not.

If things are going well, say so. If you're doubting everything you just read, admit it. The goal is a safe place for real talk.

If someone shares doubts, walk with them through what their statement says. Use scripture. Remind them that feelings shift, but truth holds steady.

Digging Up Doubt: How to Pull the Roots, Not Just the Weeds

Recurring doubts are not a sign of failure. They're a sign of growth. Ask yourself: Where do these doubts come from? Is it guilt? A past experience? A bad day?

Journaling helps. Write your questions or worries. Don't censor yourself. Add scripture next to your questions. Compare your personal feelings with declared truth.

Years ago, I dealt with feeling like I didn't measure up. I'd done everything "right," but one bad moment made me feel like a fraud. I got tired of it and wrote down everything I believed about Jesus and what He did for me. Declaring it out loud every morning rewired my default from uncertainty to assurance.

I've watched dozens do the same thing. Each has their own style. But truth, declared and repeated, beats back the emotion-driven fog almost every time.

Group Declarations: Why Saying It Together Amplifies the Effect

After the week of individual reading, gather with your group (or a friend) and recite your statements out loud. You can use your wording or create a shared version. The point is to reinforce shared identity.

Take your time. Let the words settle in. Saying it together adds weight. Hearing others declare the same truths locks in the reality that you're not alone.

Sometimes this reveals more doubts. That's good. Afterward, ask: "Did anything feel hard to say? Did any part feel fake?" Don't gloss over tough spots. These reveal areas of wounds or misunderstandings. Work through them as a group. Open scripture. Answer with truth. Remind each other that doubt is not the opposite of faith. It often leads to deeper assurance.

When Doubts Keep Showing Up: Hit Pause and Diagnose

Some doubts won't go away. Slow down and ask: What about this truth feels unworkable? Is it an old belief, a past hurt, or something unresolved?

People often trace big uncertainties to a childhood comment or old teaching. Bring it into the open. Then do something about it. Offer gentle, direct responses rooted in scripture. Keep it specific.

Don't let this become a blame game. This is about building muscle, not pretending to have arrived. Real strength is honesty plus practice.

Celebrating Wins: Why Progress, Not Perfection, Is the Real Goal

By day seven, you might feel different, or just more settled. Either way, celebrate. Take time as a group or by yourself to recognize what's changed. Share stories. Reading the statement or talking through doubts brings real shifts.

Progress can be subtle. You might doubt less. Maybe you update your statement. That's not weakness. That's ownership of your faith.

How Leaders Keep the Ball Rolling (Spoiler: It's Not by Acting Perfect)

If you're a leader or mentor, don't fake certainty. Your role is not to have all the answers but to model how to fight for clarity. Share your story. Be honest about when you felt shaken and how you found steadiness again.

Model checking in, not as a task but as a practice that builds trust. Encourage questions. Keep it personal. Help your group personalize the truth and support each other without shame.

Remind everyone why this matters. When identity is anchored, people stop living at the mercy of their moods and start helping others. That kind of leadership multiplies.

Using the Statement as a Weapon (Yes, You Read That Right)

Challenges and doubts will keep coming. The Statement of Salvation isn't a one-time fix. It's now a tool. When lies creep back in, read it out loud again. Text it to a friend. Put it on your mirror or fridge.

I've returned to mine many times. It quiets my mind, even

for a moment. Over time, truth gets louder. Doubts lose their volume.

Wrapping It All Up: Why This Changes Everything

Anchoring your identity is not a single event. It is a daily practice. Replacing emotional uncertainty with consistent truth brings peace.

This isn't just for personal security. Anchored people lead, comfort others, and live with boldness. Anchored people ride out storms without losing grip on what matters.

The Statement of Salvation offers clarity, confidence, and a shared sense of being anchored. You'll wonder how you ever managed without it.

5

Chapter 4: Unlocking Obedience: Water Baptism Commitment

What Making It Public Really Means

If you ever want to know what you actually believe, look at what you're willing to do in front of people. Most of us are great at private intentions, sure, I'll start eating kale tomorrow, just after the last donut. But the minute something gets public, all the excuses get peeled back. That's where commitment turns real, and in the case of water baptism, it isn't just about getting wet or ticking off a religious box. What you're doing is making faith visible and, honestly, a little bit scary… because real obedience always costs something. It's the place where "this is who I am now" and "this is what I'm going to show the world about my life" collide, and there's no pretending.

Obedience isn't just a private matter between you and God. It shows up in the world you actually live in, among the people who know you, watch you, and (sometimes) judge you. People use a lot of creative ways to avoid owning their faith in public. There's the "Oh, I'll keep my spiritual life private" move, and the classic "I'm not ready for that much attention yet." Most people avoid stepping out publicly because it feels risky. The risk is actually the whole point. Until you're willing to be seen obeying, you haven't fully decided who you're going to be. Baptism is the world's most straightforward way to say "I'm not hiding anymore, and I'm not apologizing for the changes God is making in me."

Why Obedience Forces The Issue

"Obedience" can sound a little old-school, like something reserved for grade school or the military. In a faith context, obedience isn't about blind rule-following. It's about trusting enough to move, even when it feels awkward or exposes you. Edwin Louis Cole once said, "Obedience is an act of faith; disobedience is the result of unbelief." This becomes clear when people say they believe in Jesus but then hesitate to let others know. The gap between believing in your head and living it out in front of people gets exposed.

Baptism fits right at the heart of that gap. It's one of those first moments where you get to prove, to yourself and everyone else, that your faith isn't just theory. It's real enough to make you act, get wet, and let a couple people snap awkward photos while you look like a drowned cat. When you schedule that baptism and make it public, you're building a habit of consistent, visible obedience. That's not just about you. Every time someone else sees you step forward, their own excuses look a little thinner.

The Power of Timelines and Deadlines

It's very easy to say, "I'll get baptized someday." "Someday" is the safe zone of procrastinators everywhere. To cement a real change in your life, you need a clear deadline, one that removes wiggle room. If you've made a new faith commitment, put your baptism on the calendar within thirty days. Yes, thirty. Not "one day." Not "after I feel more ready." Not "when the stars align and I've convinced myself I'll look good in front of a crowd." Thirty days.

The goal is to do it before your doubts and distractions build a case and talk you out of it. This isn't a suggestion for the super-spiritual. It's a practical, boots-on-the-ground way to anchor your faith in action. Get specific. Look at the calendar, talk to whoever handles the baptism schedule at your church or community, and pick a date that won't let you off the hook. You're setting a marker in your life that can't be erased or faked.

Making It a Shared Moment: Why Witnesses Matter

Some people say, "Can't I just do this on my own, quietly, with nobody watching?" That approach avoids accountability and staying anonymous. The purpose is moving faith out of your comfort zone and letting it change the stories people tell about you. Witnesses help with that. New believers should invite at least two witnesses, friends, a mentor, or a family member.

It's partly about support. Everyone feels less anxious when someone cheers for them. But it's mostly about building a habit of public faith. When those witnesses see you step in the water and come out again, you're not just getting baptized. You're giving them permission to hold you to the standard you just set. That's powerful. After you make it official, your friends, family, and even skeptical relatives now have a front-row seat to your new baseline of boldness. This makes it hard to hide or backpedal when things get tough.

The Accountability Chain Reaction

Changing anything in your life, diet, habits, even flossing, requires accountability. Baptism is the faith version of telling your whole house, "By the way, I'm not eating this anymore." It's a public line in the sand. Everyone who saw it now gets to nudge you forward instead of giving you a pass when you waver.

This isn't as intimidating as it sounds. Most people find it freeing. When the people around you expect you to keep growing, you stop spending energy on hiding or pretending. You start focusing on what's next. If you're nervous about public commitments, that's normal. The good news is that after you take the leap, your confidence grows. Baptism clarifies who you are and what you're about, not just for others, but for you.

Writing Your Faith Story, Three Quick Reflections

Don't just file the memory away and move on. After someone is baptized, they should write three short reflections. Keep them honest and raw. No bonus points for pretty words. The value comes from not letting the moment slip by. Reflect on:

1. What did public obedience mean to you, and how did it feel?
2. How has being baptized shifted your sense of identity and faith?
3. What are you hoping changes now that this step is real and public?

You don't have to write much. Just enough to process what happened. Don't trust your memory, write it down. Revisit those realizations. Let them shape what you do next. This becomes a resource for everyone who asks "What changed?" or "How did it feel?" in the future. These reflections become surprisingly valuable, especially during moments of doubt or forgetfulness.

Addressing Theological and Emotional Roadblocks

Baptism stirs up debates, fears, and strange inner dialogues. Some panic about "doing it wrong." Others worry they'll invalidate their salvation by being baptized before they feel "holy enough." Some people try to intellectualize baptism so thoroughly that the core meaning gets lost.

That's why it helps to tackle these objections in group meetings. Emotional hang-ups and theological confusion are easier to deal with in community. Sharing stories, both from early church history and real people today, helps. People two thousand years ago faced the same social pressure and jitters. Baptism isn't about earning or proving spiritual credentials. It's a sign to display what's already true inside you. It's not a test to see if you're worthy. Faith wasn't meant to stay invisible.

Role-Play: The Secret Weapon For Invitations

It can be awkward to invite someone to a baptism. Many people freeze up, unsure of how to explain it. Practice helps. Role-play the invitation in the group. It may sound cheesy, but it works.

Take turns practicing this simple invite: "Hey, I'm getting baptized in a few weeks. This matters to me, and I'd be honored if you came." Simple. Honest. No over-explaining. After a few tries, it's much easier. This builds a real-life skill. It also makes inviting others to take steps of obedience easier, whether in baptism or any other area.

The Point Is Not Transactional, It's Confirmational

Some worry that baptism is a religious transaction, like a spiritual insurance policy or a gold star. That's incorrect. Baptism does not get you saved. It confirms what God has already started inside.

It's a declaration. This principle shows up in early Christian communities and healthy faith groups today. A 2020 Assemblies of God study found that people who are baptized show greater clarity, more spiritual discipline, and a stronger sense of belonging. Those results can't be faked. Public action forces you to make up your mind and stick with it. Your mind starts shifting to match your decision.

The Power of a Prayer Circle

One last key piece: the prayer circle. When someone gets baptized in a small group, the group doesn't just say "good luck." They gather, put hands on shoulders (if that's okay), and pray.

It's not about perfect words. It's about affirming courage and asking God to anchor the next season. People walk into prayer circles nervous and walk out with resolve. Having others acknowledge your obedience out loud matters. If you've never had a group cheer you on and bless your next step, it's something to look forward to.

Cementing the Memory and Setting the Tone

Baptism isn't a blip on the radar. It's the start of a pattern. You're building obedience muscle memory. That's why it helps to share a post-baptism reflection with the group, not as a flex, but to inspire others.

These moments shape what comes next. People remember courage. They remember honesty. They remember ordinary people choosing faith over fear. Every time someone steps out, it raises the bar. Just by sharing your story, you help make it real again. You remind yourself that you belong here.

Real Faith, Real Action, And A Final Nudge

Baptism isn't for sideline sitters. It's for people ready to make a real, no-turning-back move. Don't wait until you feel spiritual or doubt-free. Decide that faith is trustworthy enough to obey, and act on it. Publicly. Boldly. With others watching.

If something inside you is arguing to delay, "Maybe next month, maybe after I get things together", that's a sign this step really matters. Discomfort signals something powerful is happening. People delay hoping fear will fade. It won't. The only way to beat fear is to act first.

Set your date. Invite your witnesses. Write your reflections. Face pushback with your group. Practice your invitations. Celebrate the step with prayer. Don't let the moment fade. Obedience will outlast your awkwardness. Every single time.

For those looking for reassurance, don't wait until you're "ready." You never will be. Don't try to make it perfect. You'll miss the point. Step in, do it in public, and let yourself be changed. That's how faith moves from your head into your life.

6

Chapter 5: Practicing Faith: The 21-Day Faith Log

Get Ready to See Faith Get Some Real-Life Muscle

I've lost count of how many times someone has told me, "I just wish my faith felt stronger day-to-day." We're all hungry for the kind of faith that doesn't flatline the second life gets loud or unpredictable. You're with me on that, right? Good. Let's get tactical.

I'm not here to sell you on another all-or-nothing spiritual sprint. I'm also not interested in the "try harder, think happier" school of advice, because that kind of stuff makes people secretly roll their eyes. What actually moves the needle? Turning belief into something you do on purpose. Something so practical you can look back after three weeks and say, "Wow. That wasn't just theory. I saw it happen."

Why Intentional Faith Is the Opposite of Wishful Thinking

People drift through years thinking spiritual growth just "happens" if you hang around church long enough or have enough inspirational quotes stuck on your fridge. That's about as effective as taping a gym membership to your mirror and

CHAPTER 5: PRACTICING FAITH: THE 21-DAY FAITH LOG

expecting your biceps to grow.

The deepest, most robust faith is built the way any skill is: deliberately, one choice at a time. I picked this up the hard way (pro tip: the hard way leaves dents), but the best shortcut I've discovered is the 21-Day Faith Log. It's simple enough for anyone to try, but there's nothing lightweight about the results. Faith moves from the background into the front row of your actual circumstances.

Taking Passive Belief and Giving It a Job

The Faith Log is a daily training ground. It's you choosing to notice, record, and build on God's faithfulness, day after day, for three straight weeks. This is not about "positive thinking." This is you inviting reality to the table and refusing to ignore the small stuff.

For years, I'd read stories of spiritual giants who seemed to get these wild, miraculous answers. Most days I was struggling just to remember what I was supposed to be believing for. The breakthrough came when I decided to pay attention, intentionally, with a notebook and pen, and make it a habit. When faith feels theoretical, the Faith Log helps you see what happens when you actually log the proof.

Setting Up Your 21-Day Faith Log, No Overthinking Allowed

Grab any notebook you won't lose (the back of a bill, your phone's notes app, or a fancy journal, whatever keeps you coming back every day). We're going for "used daily," not "Instagram perfect." Set aside a little time each morning and evening. If you're a night owl, shift it later. The point is consistency, not clock-watching.

Now, here's the morning drill:

- Each morning, pick one specific promise from Scripture.

Don't get paralyzed flipping through pages. Scan for one that matches what you're facing, provision, courage, peace, whatever feels raw and real.
- Read the promise out loud. No mumbling. There's power in hearing yourself declare it, even if at first you feel sheepish.
- Jot down the promise. Writing it helps your brain hold on to it, and gives you something to look back at on the tough days.

That's it for the morning. Move through your day as usual, but keep your eyes peeled for any sign, big or tiny, that connects to that promise. Don't overanalyze. Don't set up secret criteria for what counts. The goal is to notice something, not to give yourself another spiritual class to fail.

The Nightly Check-In: Where the Real Proof Shows Up

Every evening, before bed, while dinner simmers, or during that five-minute lull before scrolling your phone, open your Faith Log. Ask: Did I spot any evidence of God's faithfulness related to today's promise? Don't wait for a thunderclap. The most significant progress usually looks ordinary at first.

Some days, "evidence" might look like someone sharing a kind word, a bill getting unexpectedly paid, or just the fact that anxiety dialed down a notch. Frequently, it's a subtle shift in your mood, a conversation that hit the spot, or finding courage when you normally wouldn't.

Write it down, even if you think, "Is this too small to mention?" There's no such thing as "too small" when you're learning to recognize God moving. Over the weeks, these "small" notices pile up into a huge wall of confidence.

There's No 'Failing', Only Tracking Progress

Some days you'll forget, feel unmotivated, or wonder if any

of this is working. A lot of people bail: they miss a day or two, and that inner critic pipes up with, "See, you're not cut out for this." Ignore that voice. Progress isn't perfection. If you miss a day, jump back in. If you feel silly recording what seems like a "minor" thing, remember, faith grows when you water it. Small roots go deep over time. Missed a step? That's not a crisis. It's a normal part of starting anything new.

If you get discouraged, look back at what you've recorded since day one. Still blank? Ask a friend in your group to swap stories for a night. You'll be surprised at how quickly you start noticing more, just by being around others trying to do the same.

Leaders Go First, Modeling What Matters

If you're in a leadership role, a group, a class, even an informal circle, don't just give directions from the sidelines. Do the Faith Log yourself. Share your actual entries (yes, even the "I almost forgot tonight" ones). People learn most by seeing vulnerability in action, not hearing polished stories that sound like they were airbrushed for a church newsletter.

There's more breakthrough in groups where leaders fumble their way through, admit doubts, and write about the tiniest "answers" than in a dozen classes focused on theory. When you model what daily faith looks like with all its starts, stops, and restarts, others relax. They realize growth is messy, not magic.

And if you're terrible at consistency? Say so. Don't stay there. Invite the group to hold you accountable, even poke fun when you slack off. Shared humanity beats fake perfection every time.

Weekly Sharing: Boosts, Laughs, and the Power of "Me Too"

Every week, set aside time for the group to swap Faith Log highlights. Don't restrict it to the jaw-dropping stuff. Some of the best moments come from the "is this even spiritual?" discoveries. Encouragement multiplies when someone shares how an awkward situation worked out, or when another admits they almost gave up, then caught a glimmer of hope anyway.

When people hear real, honest stories of noticing God at work, it normalizes victory and struggle. It makes everyone braver about looking for evidence, big or small. Accountability isn't code for pressure. It's a built-in support system that helps you push through those days when you'd rather binge TV than focus on faith.

When Small Things Add Up: The Unexpected Breakthroughs

Logging "just okay" moments toys with your expectations. At first, most folks struggle to even spot clues that God is involved in their regular routines. But give it a week or so, and the brain starts searching. Suddenly, that minor win you logged last Thursday looks a lot like the start of a bigger pattern.

This effect isn't wishful thinking. It's brain training. You're literally rewiring your habits to expect reliability from God, not just random luck.

Troubleshooting: What If I Don't 'Feel' Anything?

Some days, the sky won't part, and you'll wonder, "Am I imagining things?" That's normal. Faith isn't always a firework show. If you don't see anything obvious, review your day for any little bump up from what you expected. Did you stay calm in traffic? Did a situation get resolved that usually drags on? Even the absence of drama counts.

If you're still drawing a blank, flip through earlier entries. Sometimes, gratitude shows up in the rearview mirror. Or reach out to a fellow log-keeper, a five-minute chat can jog your memory or reframe your perspective. The process isn't about forcing emotional highs. It's about catching reality in the act. You're not here to manufacture proof. You're here to notice what's already been happening under the surface.

After 21 Days: Building Your Own "Remembering Stones"

Once you hit day 21, don't skip the celebration. Get everyone together (snacks recommended) and go around sharing the top three moments where faith got more real or God's faithfulness blindsided you. Don't worry about impressing anyone. The gold is in the stories where you least expected help, or where old fears shrank just a bit.

This isn't about closing the log and forgetting it happened. These entries are your set of "remembering stones", something you can come back to the next time life throws a curveball. Each note in your log is evidence stacked up for future battles. You're creating a personal faith database, ready to squash "what if" worries before they get loud.

If you're feeling ambitious, challenge yourself (or your group) to keep the habit going the next time a crisis hits. This isn't a one-off experiment. It's a toolkit for every trial ahead.

Keeping the Momentum: What to Do Next

Momentum loves company. If you want the Faith Log to stick, team up with someone who's just as stubborn about not quitting. Trade updates, laugh off the awkward days, and give each other permission to celebrate baby steps.

Annoyed by the idea of more "tasks?" Flip it. Tell yourself you're just collecting a weird set of stories you'll want to laugh about next month. You're not trying to score spiritual points. You're creating reminders that faith isn't a one-week wonder.

If you're leading others, rotate who shares first each week, and don't spot-clean your stories to look better than you are. The more honest you are about your own slow progress, the more you let others breathe.

Why This Matters for the Long Haul

Not every person who tries the Faith Log has an instant

breakthrough. Like any daily practice, some days you'll feel like nothing is changing. You're rewiring what you expect, not chasing quick fixes. You're building a well-worn path of trust for when life gets brutal later.

Years from now, when you're tempted to panic or doubt, you'll have a backlog of moments where God came through. Faith grows not by collecting mountaintop stories, but by stacking up daily, often unremarkable, wins. That's how spiritual confidence goes from fragile to unshakeable.

Final Thoughts: No Magic. Just Movement.

Nobody drifts into deep faith by accident. You get there one day at a time by showing up, writing it down, and refusing to discount the tiny victories. Skip the urge to chase perfection or make your log entries look impressive. The whole point is to catch faith doing its work right in the mess and monotony of daily life.

Three weeks from today, look up, you'll be surprised at how much evidence you've collected. Not because your life suddenly got easier, but because you decided to stop missing what was already happening.

If you're tired of second-guessing whether faith "works," this is your invitation: stop guessing. Start logging.

7

Chapter 6: Getting Real About Faith's First Steps

Q: What if I finish my "salvation statement," but honestly, I just don't feel changed, like salvation hasn't "clicked" for me?

A: I get this one a lot, and it's totally normal to second-guess yourself after putting words to something so huge. Now, about those feelings, they're like weather in April, changing by the hour. Today you may feel nothing, tomorrow something different. The truth, though, never shifts depending on mood or nerves. According to Romans 10:9-10, faith sits anchored in what Christ did, not how your heart plays tricks. Faith isn't some fuzzy emotion that drifts by, it's a reality grounded in God's own words. If you wake up tomorrow and still don't "feel" saved, speak the truth anyway. Read your statement out loud again. Sometimes it takes weeks, months...sometimes it never lines up perfectly. That's completely fine. What matters is that you're reminding yourself, again and again, that your new identity stands on what Christ has finished, not on the echoes of last night's doubts. I've had entire seasons where it all felt hollow, but the foundation didn't move. You keep walking, even when you're slogging through the mud. That's faith showing up, even if you're tired of waiting for your heart to catch up.

Q: I said the sinner's prayer earlier. Isn't that the main thing? Do I actually need to get baptized quickly?

A: This one can get a little tense in a church lobby. Maybe you've heard people say "the prayer" and call it good, like that's the magical step. I know the urge to treat it as a kind of finish line. But if you really look close at the pattern in the New Testament, baptism comes right after faith. Sometimes people didn't even wait a day. Acts 2:38 doesn't describe it as a helpful suggestion or a ritual for later. It's a direct command from Peter's first big sermon. Jesus never asks for delayed obedience. Baptism isn't a bonus track. It marks the start of your new life, stamping your story in public. If you wait around "until it feels right" or try to perfect yourself first, you're missing the entire point. The urgency isn't about pressure. It's about aligning your outside with what already changed inside. Waiting months or years isn't safer. It can leave you stuck, half-in with your new identity but not living it out. Get it on the calendar now, even if you're nervous. That first obedient act, the plunge itself, tells your heart, your friends, and even your future doubts: nothing is holding me back anymore.

Q: But can't faith just grow on its own as life goes along? Maybe it'll just happen if I chill out and wait?

A: Coasting is tempting. Maybe you've seen people drift into deeper faith like it happened by accident. Sometimes, from the outside, it might look that way, but there's always more under the surface. Colossians 2:6-7 shows faith as something to walk out on purpose, step by step. The "natural" growth comes after intentional planting and tending. Nobody drifts into maturity by accident. If someone says it's all automatic, they're skipping

CHAPTER 6: GETTING REAL ABOUT FAITH'S FIRST STEPS

the hard parts: the daily choices, small course corrections, the determination to hang on, especially when nothing makes sense. Faith doesn't just trickle in. It grows when you lean in, take action, and keep wrestling with God's truth in real life. Picture it like caring for a stubborn plant. It only thrives with attention, sunlight, water, and sometimes a bit of pruning. Letting things slide means you get spiritual weeds, not fruit.

Q: How soon is too soon to schedule baptism? If I don't feel totally ready, do I need to wait?

A: Every new believer second-guesses the timing. The idea that you need to feel "ready" is one of those tricky half-truths that keep people stuck for years. Baptism, by design, is meant to come right at the start, not after you've figured everything out. There's no secret knowledge or hidden emotional switch that makes you "officially" ready. The only thing that matters is you've trusted Christ. That's it. The earliest Christians barely got dry before they jumped in. They didn't stall for months sorting out every possible doubt. Every hour you wait is one more hour letting fear call the shots. The moment you know you're following Jesus, the sooner you get baptized the more you cement that reality, for yourself, your family, everyone watching. "Schedule as soon as possible" isn't blunt. It's freeing. It removes endless waiting, excuses, or the imaginary line of "good enough." The longer you hold off, the more you let uncertainty build walls, and those walls are a pain to tear down later.

Q: What if I skip some days in my faith log, or I go through a lazy stretch, am I blowing my shot at spiritual growth?

A: If you're the sort who starts strong and fizzles after a week, welcome to the club. Missing days, losing momentum, staring at a blank journal page...been there. You don't fail God's test by missing a few check-ins. The real loss comes from giving up completely. God isn't grading you on a streak or giving out gold stars for perfect attendance. Progress matters more than perfection. He's looking for a real relationship, not a spotless chart. If you miss a day, just start again, next morning, or whenever you remember. Each time you return, you're making a statement: my story isn't over, and I refuse to let mistakes define me. Over time, that kind of grit builds deeper roots than any perfect record ever could. Miss a week, a month, or a year? The answer is always the same, pick it up again. God isn't keeping score the way we think.

Q: Why bother with all these "daily faith actions" if I already believe in Jesus? Isn't that overkill?

A: Regular, intentional steps don't shrink your faith into busywork. They rescue it from drifting into the background. When you write down what God's doing, pray on purpose, or look for what He's up to in the ordinary stuff, that's where you notice faith turning real. Relationships that matter always get your time and attention. Daily actions aren't about earning anything. They show what's valuable. The more often you step in with intention, the more chances you give God to show up in everyday moments. It's not overkill. It's oxygen.

Q: I'm worried I'll never feel the relief or joy people talk about, what if this all stays dry and mechanical for me?

A: Many believers keep going without fireworks or huge breakthroughs. That's not a failure. Sometimes joy and relief feel far away, maybe even reserved for someone "holier" or more emotional. Faith stays anchored even when your mood won't budge. You choose to keep coming back, repeating the truth, and plugging away at the habits. Over time, you rewire expectations. Maybe it'll always feel a little dry. But

CHAPTER 6: GETTING REAL ABOUT FAITH'S FIRST STEPS

in unexpected ways, you'll look back and see your roots grew deeper. Sometimes the breakthrough is realizing you're still here, still coming back. That's saying something. Steady faith is underrated.

Q: What happens if I make a public stand and then mess up? Won't people call me a hypocrite if I blow it after baptism?

A: Public mess-ups don't disqualify you. Taking bold steps like baptism or sharing your story doesn't require perfection. It shows you're trusting God, not yourself. You'll stumble. Sometimes, it'll be spectacular. That's expected. If you fall down, you get back up. People don't need to see flawless performance. They need to see real change and honest recovery. Mistakes don't erase commitment. They give new chances to live it out publicly. In the end, consistency isn't about never failing. It's about how many times you choose to start again. Starting again proves this whole thing is real.

Q: Why does baptism have to be so public? I'd rather keep my journey to myself.

A: It's tempting to keep something this personal hidden, especially if you're not showy. But baptism puts your faith where it can be seen, not just by others, but by yourself. It locks in your decision, marks your old life as finished, and stamps your new start. You're not performing. You're letting people witness your transformation. The ripple effect reaches farther than you expect. Your openness gives others permission to take their own steps. Public steps build courage you can't get by staying hidden. You might feel exposed, but you end up with a stronger support system cheering you along.

Q: Is it really possible to grow faith by just "seeing God at work," or is that wishful thinking?

A: You won't always recognize God's work in the moment.

It's easy to call it coincidence or forget last week's prayers. But when you pay attention, write things down, remember the little ways God provides, you start noticing what you used to miss. Daily habits and logs aren't for impressing anyone. They train your mind to see what's already there. Over time, these tiny moments add up. You catch yourself saying, "That wasn't just luck." Even if you slip or forget to look, you can always circle back. The more you look, the more you see. One "aha" moment often sparks another.

Q: Does God really honor progress over perfection, or am I just making excuses for myself?

A: Lowering the bar too far means nothing changes. Progress over perfection doesn't mean "do nothing and call it a win." But in real life, with doubts and stumbles, God isn't keeping a failure tally. He pays attention to movement, not flawless execution. It's actually harder this way, because you have to keep choosing to get back up. Scripture shows that God works with people in process. He meets you on the road. The only ones who don't move forward are the ones who quit. As long as you're still showing up, God's not finished. Progress doesn't always look pretty, but it moves you closer.

Q: If I really believe all this, why is it still such a struggle to do the daily faith actions?

A: Faith habits don't get easy. Most of the time, struggle means you're doing something real. Habits don't feel natural at first. You have to keep choosing them until they're part of your life. Waiting for it to feel automatic often means nothing happens. Struggle means you're moving against the current, not drifting. God uses those tough days to shape character and build endurance. The people who keep showing up, bored, frustrated, uncertain, are often the ones who find depth later.

CHAPTER 6: GETTING REAL ABOUT FAITH'S FIRST STEPS

Struggle isn't failure. It's practice.

Q: What if my friends or family think I'm taking all this "first steps" stuff way too seriously?

A: Getting intentional about faith can make other people uncomfortable. They might roll their eyes, joke about your "phase," or get annoyed. Most big changes meet pushback, especially meaningful ones. Downplaying your start to fit in risks missing what's possible. Over time, the same people who scoffed may be the first to ask questions when life gets hard. You're not looking for approval. You're choosing to make faith real. Stand your ground. The payoff comes later, and it's bigger than expected.

Q: Is it okay if I sometimes worry that this whole journey is too much for me?

A: Honest worry is part of the package. You might feel overwhelmed, doubt your ability to keep up, or wonder if you're faking it. Real steps expose limits and fears. Admit them. Tell God, tell someone you trust. Saying it out loud shrinks fear. Pretending you don't struggle is what gets in the way. Faith grows when you drag doubts into the light.

Q: If I lose momentum and fall back into old habits, is that it for me?

A: No. Every believer's story includes restarts, detours, and disappointment. No one does this perfectly. The difference is they didn't stay down. Falling into old habits doesn't end your story. It sets up a stronger comeback. Some of the strongest faith grows from someone's third, fifth, or twentieth restart. The only failure is not getting up. Don't beat yourself up. Start again, even if you've lost count.

Q: Will doing all this change my sense of who I am? Or will I always feel like the same old person underneath?

A: Change usually happens slowly. Over time, you'll find yourself thinking and reacting differently before you even notice it. The most important shifts sneak up on you. You'll see how you handle stress, how your priorities change, how fear loses its grip. Daily changes may be invisible to you, but others will notice. Your new identity in Christ isn't decoration, it reshapes how you live. Keep showing up, and those changes will take root.

Right now, these first steps might feel awkward, forced, or vulnerable. That means you're in the middle of real change. Every honest question and quiet restart moves you forward. You're right where you need to be.

8

Chapter 7: Realigning Your Core Foundations

Alright, let's press pause and actually look at where we've landed so far. This is a recap, a check-in, not a rehash. So just to be clear, you're not about to re-read things you just worked through. Instead, I'm laying it all out, what's shifted, what stands out, and how you can move forward with a sense of clarity and security.

You're carrying a toolkit now that you didn't have ten, twenty, maybe even two pages ago. And honestly, I know that just because something's been covered, it doesn't mean it's instantly clicked or permanently changed how you live. That's fine. Seeing where the journey has taken you, though, is a real step most people skip, usually because they're too busy chasing the next thing. But we're not doing that. So here we go.

The Building Blocks: What We Set in Place

First up, the whole point of this section was simple: lay down the core blocks for a faith that can take a hit and not even wobble. We dove into what I called the initial pillars, salvation, baptism, and taking real, tangible faith steps. Now, if you raced through these earlier, this is a good moment to slow down just a notch.

Why did we start there? Because everything else depends on getting this part right. You've seen how anchoring your identity in unchanging truth gives you a rock to stand on even when everything else feels up for grabs. That's not just theory either. This becomes the stable ground for every single part of your growth from here on out.

Experiencing clarity and security in your own salvation doesn't just help you sleep better at night. It also keeps you steady when life, emotions, or even well-meaning people try to yank out your roots. There's nothing fluffy about it. Without this anchor, the rest of the journey never really gets off the ground.

Most folks trip up early by relying more on feelings than on grounded, biblical truth. Feelings are sneaky like that. We also tend to put off baptism, or treat it as an add-on instead of a direct command. Then, there's the mistake of skipping all those small, daily actions that actually grow genuine faith, waiting for some emotional high to do the heavy lifting instead.

If you spotted yourself in any of that, congratulations. You're in good company. It means your radar is working.

The Identity Anchor: Statement of Salvation

Then came the turning point, writing your own Statement of Salvation. You might remember sitting down and trying to put into words exactly what Jesus did, how you responded, and most importantly, what that means for your identity now. Putting pen to paper on this isn't just a box to check. It's a reset for your mind and spirit.

Did you sign and date it? Even better, did you actually read it out loud to yourself every morning for a week, like I told you to? A bunch of people reading this probably meant to, then forgot after the first day. It's easy to let routines slip. That's why I stressed daily check-ins (and yes, sometimes a bit of leader-driven encouragement or correction).

When the doubts started popping up, which is almost guaranteed, the next step wasn't to shove them aside. Bring them out, stack them up against what the Bible actually promises, and let the truth do the heavy lifting. Maybe you journaled some of your questions, maybe you read Romans 8:16 with fresh eyes, or maybe you just heard someone else's story of wrestling and found some freedom.

Community mattered here, too. Telling the truth together, out loud, made it a shared reality, not just a private one. Declaring your salvation as a group? That's not just for show. There's something about hearing others say what you believe that makes it stick even deeper. And troubleshooting doubts as a group, armed with Scripture, meant you didn't have to figure it all out on your own.

Finishing the seven days, I asked you to celebrate progress, not perfection. Maybe you found yourself surprised by what happened in those seven days, maybe not. Either way, the foundation is poured. This is one of those tools you'll want to pull out again when the pressure's on.

Taking Action: Water Baptism Commitment

Next, baptism. I pushed for urgency here, getting baptized within thirty days of deciding to follow Jesus. That probably felt fast to some, and maybe uncomfortable to others, especially if you grew up thinking baptism was optional or only for people who "feel ready." Obedience is rarely about comfort, and even less about waiting for perfect timing.

Gathering at least two witnesses to be present made it public, not private. That accountability might feel like a risk, but it's really just honesty. Afterward, writing three short reflections about what this step meant for your faith and your identity turned a quick event into a lasting memory.

If objections showed up, whether theological ("Does this really matter?"), emotional ("Am I really qualified?"), or just plain nerves, they got addressed out loud. We looked at early church stories and swapped testimonies in the group. That wasn't just background noise. Modeling invitations and even role-playing how to ask someone else to get baptized helped shift everything from theory to actual, everyday life.

And that prayer circle at the end? Some of you probably thought it was cheesy or uncomfortable. But praying together for courage and lifelong boldness, then sharing your reflections with the group, solidified something that just can't happen if you keep your faith steps hidden. It set the tone for what comes next. These aren't isolated experiences, they stack up.

Living Faith: The 21-Day Faith Log

This last piece, your 21-Day Faith Log, is where all the theory met daily practice. It's one thing to talk about faith, nod along, and even agree that God is working. It's another thing entirely to take a promise from Scripture every morning, say it out loud where you can actually hear it, then at night write down what evidence you saw (even when it felt tiny, or you had to really squint to spot it).

I shared my own examples for a reason: sometimes, you need someone else to show you what "noticing God's work" actually looks like day-to-day. Watching for God's faithfulness isn't about tallying up only the big moments. It's about seeing progress, however subtle, and refusing to let discouragement call the shots.

If you missed a day or got discouraged because your examples seemed "too small," I get it. But the point was always progress, not hitting some pretend perfection milestone. Sharing your findings weekly built real encouragement and group accountability, another layer of proof that you're not imagining it, and you're not alone.

When the 21 days wrapped up, I challenged everyone to pick out three moments where God just showed up unexpectedly or your confidence in Him shifted. Those "remembering stones", as I call them, are the kind of thing you'll keep coming back to during the rougher seasons.

If you're wondering whether you'll ever stop doubting... probably not. But you now have a rhythm for remembering, a path for pushing through, and a team to help you not forget what's true when your memory gets fuzzy.

What Shifted (Even If You Didn't Notice)

The shifts might feel subtle or obvious. Either's fine. You don't have to pretend everything changed overnight. But now, you have tools for:

- Anchoring your identity in something that lasts, not in whatever you happen to feel this morning.
- Seeing salvation as settled fact, not a moving target based on how well you performed today.
- Taking action when it comes to obedience, especially with baptism, turning theory into commitment, private faith into public declaration.
- Building a pattern of faith that doesn't wait for "big" moments, but grabs hold of each day, even when the evidence seems small.
- Using community for truth and encouragement, not just for group activities or checklists.

If you ever notice yourself slipping back into waiting on feelings, or putting off action, or isolating instead of sharing... just know, it happens. That's why we set these foundations in the first place. You're not meant to muscle through change alone or try to guess your way forward.

You can now spot these basic mistakes as soon as they start to show up. You'll spend way less time getting stuck. Recognizing them is the first step to responding differently next time they pop up.

So, What's Next?

Don't ditch this recap just because you think you "know it already." The people who get the furthest are the ones who revisit the basics most often. Not because they're slow, but because they know that old lessons matter most in new situations.

You've got a foundation that'll actually hold, for real, not just in theory. Now, we're about to see that solid ground get put to the test.

...

Next section? Here's a taste of what's around the corner:

- Moving beyond basics: We'll dig into discipleship, the power of the Holy Spirit, and what it takes to make your faith contagious (not just personal).
- Common pitfalls: See how missing accountability, ignoring your spiritual gifts, or ducking evangelism can totally stall out your growth.
- Group momentum: Get the inside track on establishing a 90-Day Growth Plan that isn't boring or busywork.
- Spiritual gifts, unboxed: What happens when you stop benching your gifts and actually use them? We're going

to find out.
- Evangelism gets a rebrand: The BLESS Evangelism Challenge will show you that reaching others isn't reserved for the "super spiritual" or outgoing types.

So, don't zone out. If you thought foundation was important, the next part is where faith becomes action, community, and movement. Let's see what happens when you put it all together.

9

Chapter 8: From Foundations to Fruit: Growing and Multiplying Disciples

"If you can't describe what you're doing as a process, you don't know what you're doing." – W. Edwards Deming

It started for me the day I realized following Jesus wasn't meant to be a static, private routine. There was a morning, ordinary, gray, maybe a little chilly if I'm honest... I stared at the ceiling and caught myself thinking, "Is this all there is?" Each week rolled by with the same prayers, same hopes for growth, but the sense of movement in my faith? Missing in action. I'd hear people talk about discipleship, using big church words, and it always seemed like something reserved for the "pro" Christians, the ones who had all the answers, wore tidy shirts, read the footnotes in their Bibles just for fun. Not me. At least, that's how it felt.

For a while, I just kept circling around. Go to church. Try to do the right thing. Smile at someone in the grocery store. Maybe invite someone to a worship night (and almost hope they said no because, well, what if they asked tough questions?). Looking back, that sort of drifting wasn't the problem. It was the symptom. No real process, no clear next steps, and nothing keeping me accountable except a vague sense of "should."

Things changed when I stopped waiting for someone else to hand me the magic blueprint. I started asking, "What if growth is supposed to look a lot more like a garden than an assembly line?" Not perfect, not always neat, but deeply alive. Sometimes messy, sometimes surprising, and definitely interactive. Discipleship isn't just a fancy word for an organized gathering. It's real life, real people, actual grit, uncomfortable honesty, and stories that never quite go according to script. You build something with your own hands, you water it, you watch it grow, or sometimes wilt... then you try again with a little more wisdom (and sometimes a little more stubbornness).

The Secret Ingredient Nobody Talks About

When I dug into what actually moves the needle in following Jesus, it wasn't fancy programs or clever slogans. It was the Holy Spirit, active, present, persistent. Not in a "do this or else" kind of way, but more like the friend who sticks around when everyone else heads home. If you've ever tried to muster up spiritual courage when your tank's running dry, that just doesn't work for long. At some point, self-discipline doesn't cut it.

You need power. The kind that doesn't just push you to change a few behaviors, but lights a fire inside you that other people notice. And yes, people notice, because Spirit-empowered change looks different. It's unpredictable, often inconvenient, and sometimes incredibly fun. I can't count how many times I've seen quiet, overlooked folks come alive when they finally believe that the Spirit actually wants to use them, not just the "outgoing" ones. That's because this isn't about personality. It's about being available.

The longer I tried to systematize spiritual growth, the more I came back to basic things. Listening for the Spirit's nudge, as awkward as that sometimes feels. Moving toward people instead of away from them. Risking a conversation that might land flat. Sometimes having absolutely no idea what I'm doing... but trusting that's enough to get started.

Discipleship, Not as a Theory, But as a Lifestyle

A lot of people get tripped up thinking discipleship is a class or a checklist. Somebody once asked me for my "step-by-step" and I nearly laughed. Mainly because I don't have one. What I've found is more like a rhythm. It starts with intentionality, making real decisions to seek growth, not just wait for it to happen by accident. Then it turns into practice, actually using your spiritual gifts, even when you're half-sure you don't have any. Most folks don't even know what their gifts are until they're already knee-deep in the chaos of community, fumbling around, trying stuff out.

Now, this part gets overlooked. Most of the time, discovery of your gifts isn't a eureka moment. More like, "Well, I tried teaching, but the kids started eating the crayons. Maybe I'll try serving behind the scenes next time." Or someone tells you that your encouragement made a difference, and you realize, oh, maybe that's something God wants to use.

Who gets to multiply disciples? Anyone willing to let their faith out of the box. If waiting to feel "ready" is the strategy, you'll probably still be waiting this time next year. I've watched unlikely people take small risks, sometimes with knees knocking, and find themselves in the middle of someone else's story of faith. There's this subtle irony. The people who see the biggest growth almost never think they're the most qualified.

Evangelism Without the Weird

Let's talk about the scariest word in church circles: evangelism. I'll admit, for a long time, that word felt loaded, like something extroverts do with bullhorns at the beach. Most folks, myself included, have tried a version of it that felt forced, awkward, or, worst-case, staged. There was a season where I tried handing out tracts at the park. Nobody ever called the number on the back. If sharing your faith feels like an unwanted sales pitch, you're not alone.

Real change happens when evangelism becomes an outflow of genuine relationship. You look for ways to serve, to listen, to show up. Sometimes it's a conversation over coffee, or maybe a simple prayer with a friend who's having a rough go. None of that requires special training. All it takes is willingness to act on small nudges, even if you're unsure how it'll go. Over time, you see God showing up in places you never expected. You notice how ordinary moments, sharing a story, offering help, even admitting your own mess, turn into seeds that take root in someone else's life. Some seeds sprout quickly, some take forever, and some get trampled. You plant again anyway.

The Power of Process (Even When It's Unpredictable)

Deming's quote about process isn't just for engineers. It's an invitation to get real about what's happening under the surface. Growth, empowerment, and multiplication don't just "happen" out of nowhere. Every person who's ever moved forward in their faith had to commit to a direction before they knew the whole map. Intentional growth means setting your sights on something and taking action, even if your steps aren't perfect or easy to diagram.

Experiencing that kind of steady, intentional movement won't make you a "super Christian." It makes you a real one. Every time you try, every time you ask God for help, you're growing. That's the difference between drifting and moving on purpose. And as you keep going, you turn around one day and realize, you're a person who does this now. The journey isn't about flawless technique. It's about persistence, humility, and learning when to rest and when to push forward (with a little laughter along the way, because you need it).

Empowerment starts when you stop waiting for permission and start using what you already have. Not to impress anyone, but to serve. For me, that looked like saying yes to small things: hosting a group, praying with someone after service, inviting one more person into my home. It wasn't glamorous, but there's an odd satisfaction in seeing someone else flourish because you created a little space for them to try, fail, and try again.

Multiplication matters because it's the one surefire way to tell if a process is real. If what you're doing stops with you, it's probably not the real thing. But when others catch on, when faith spreads, gifts get discovered, and people start serving out of their own calling, you see how wild and unpredictable God's plan for growth really is. You'll get to watch disciples make disciples. Sometimes, you'll barely recognize the people they become (in a good way).

Why This Chapter Matters Now, and for What's Next

There's a temptation. You want a formula, a shortcut, or maybe a checklist that guarantees success. What you actually need is a process that keeps you moving, learning, and failing forward, because that's where the fruit is. If you stick around for what's ahead, you'll learn how to grow, and how to multiply that growth in others (and maybe even surprise yourself in the process).

Here's what's coming: ways to experience ongoing, intentional growth without getting lost in endless theory. Practical steps to empower every believer, because nobody gets sidelined here. And a fresh take on multiplying disciples that doesn't require you to become someone you're not.

If you've been waiting for permission to get in the game, this is your invitation. Stop circling the same mountains and start walking in a new direction. One honest, Spirit-powered, sometimes awkward, often beautiful step at a time. Ready or not, it's time to get growing.

10

Chapter 9: Real Growth Needs a Real Plan

The Art of Practical Discipleship in Motion

Most Christians nod along when you mention "discipleship," but ask people how it actually happens, watch the vague hand-waving start. I've seen it myself. People toss around words like "community," "spiritual gifts," or "witnessing," but when it comes time for action, confusion crops up. You might feel lost, too, even if you've led groups or served in ministry for years. That's because church culture typically celebrates a weekly rhythm that's heavy on hearing but light on doing. If you're ready to move past theory and step into consistent growth, you'll need more than a few nice intentions or a one-off event.

Real discipleship only starts to work when you add structure, activate gifts, and actually invite people to do what scares them... evangelism included. It's not magic, and it never was.

Unstructured Christianity: Why Most People Stay Stuck

An easy mistake is chasing spiritual maturity alone. It sounds noble, "me and Jesus against the world", but it falls flat. I've sat across from dozens of people who can talk theology, but their lives show up with the same issues, month after month. They have no real plan. No one walks with them or holds them to anything beyond good intentions. Church traditions talk up the lone prophet, but the early movement of Jesus never functioned that way. Martin Luther's Small Catechism and John Wesley's class meetings didn't just hope for growth. They built a process. Meetings happened. Questions got answered. Struggles didn't get brushed aside. That rhythm created contagious energy. Results followed.

When scattered half-heartedly, spiritual disciplines hardly ever take root. If your idea of accountability is a check-in text every quarter, good luck. If you expect to "just know" when your spiritual gifts are needed, expect missed chances. I've seen longtime believers sit on their gifts for decades. Weeks pile up, nobody invites them to lead or serve, and eventually, the spark fizzles.

Some folks believe the Holy Spirit works best when we stick to "spontaneous." I used to laugh, until I watched group after group stall out because no one wanted to do the basic work of planning. Spontaneity is fun for a party, but it won't replace a plan when the goal is lasting maturity.

Community Alone Isn't Enough... But Structure Changes the Game

People gather, sing, maybe discuss a passage, then disappear. It feels like community, but it never hits the level where lives press together enough to cause friction or real transformation. Spiritual gifts, for example, often end up as random quizzes or lists in a workbook. That's it. I've seen people discover "I have the gift of encouragement!" and then nothing changes.

But with a plan for gathering, sharing, and serving together, something changes. Meeting every week feels like work at first.

(And the pushback starts immediately: "I barely have time for anything as it is!") But after a month or two, the rhythm settles in. People start to look forward to it. If you've ever belonged to a group where folks share honestly, pray, and then show up week after week for each other, you know there's a stubborn kind of joy in that. Hebrews 10:24-25 reminds us to keep meeting together and encouraging one another. That rhythm matters.

Structure isn't about control. It's about creating space for the Holy Spirit to work, not just in theory, but in annoying, beautiful, real-world ways. I've watched people who swore they'd never pray out loud eventually lead prayers that moved others to tears. I've seen introverts in the back of the room discover gifts of wisdom, hospitality, or discernment, gifts that stay buried unless someone calls them out and gives them space to grow.

Martin Luther and John Wesley both recognized that casual, "whenever we feel like it" faith rarely survives struggle. Steady meetings, paired mentoring, and accountability create an environment where faith has to move. It grows legs and stands up. Christianity Today reported in 2023 that about 60% of pastors find their small group strategy scattered and random. That's why a clear, repeatable process matters. Vagueness breeds vagueness. Clarity, repetition, and accountability build boldness.

Gifted to Serve... Not to Sit

Spiritual gifts aren't optional. 1 Corinthians 12:7 makes it clear: every believer has been handed something, for the sake of others. Still, many Christians dismiss themselves as "average." They say, "I'm not a leader, I'm not musical, I'm not good at talking to strangers," and move on. Others get excited about spiritual gifts but only use them when it's easy or expected.

Spiritual gifts exist for service. They aren't meant to make you feel special or unique. If you only focus on figuring out your gift, but never use it to serve others, you're hiding the very thing God intended to light up your community.

There's Amy. She figured out she had a teaching gift, but let it collect dust for years because she thought, "that's just for pastors." Or Marcus, always quick with a joke. He never realized his humor helped break tension in small groups and let shy people open up. Some talents seem spiritual. Others feel ordinary. All become powerful in service.

Watching people withdraw when their gifts are dismissed is disheartening. If group leaders get all the attention while those with mercy or hospitality get overlooked, people start wondering if they even matter. Community rhythms must make space for the less dramatic gifts. Otherwise, church shrinks to superstar performers and quiet spectators.

Some churches respond with a "gift drive", run everyone through an inventory and hope people self-organize. That rarely works. Others over-schedule and burn people out. The answer is much simpler. Create steady opportunities for discovery, encouragement, feedback, and experiments. I've told someone, "Try it! We'll help if it bombs." Those awkward, small, sometimes disastrous moments knit a community together. Fail together. Laugh together. Suddenly, gifts become muscle memory.

Evangelism Without the Manipulation or Awkwardness

Bringing up evangelism makes some folks twitch. There's baggage. Forced conversations, door-knocking horror stories, or awkward "God talks" in coffee shops. I've been there. More than once, I hesitated, wondering if sharing would come off fake or weird.

Evangelism works better when focused on trust, service, and presence. The BLESS model shifts the conversation. Instead of selling Jesus, it invites us to listen, eat together, serve, and share honestly when the door opens. It's more about presence than pressure.

Evangelism gets easier the more you do it. First time feels like cold water. Second time's still uncomfortable, but not as much. With practice and decent training, it shifts from "that's for experts" to "I could give it a shot." Weekly small groups become training grounds. Mess up? You get help. Succeed a little? Everyone celebrates.

People often say, "evangelism feels manipulative." That concern makes sense. Nobody wants to be "that" Christian. But when you serve and love without agenda, people notice. They ask questions when they're ready. You just need to be around when they do.

The Biggest Mistakes: No Plan, No Push, No Progress

Most groups never grow because they lack rhythm or accountability. They miss one meeting, then two. Nobody checks in. Days turn into weeks, then the group fizzles.

Another mistake is keeping spiritual gifts theoretical. People don't know how to use or develop them. So the gifted never find their groove.

Then there's evangelism. It gets written off as "for the few" or shelved after one awkward attempt.

A subtler mistake is groups that become exclusive. They turn inward, circle the wagons, and forget to invite others. The spark dies. The energy disappears.

Some think this all sounds too time-consuming. Structure actually saves time. When groups meet weekly, there's no need to chase people down or re-explain everything. Routine clears the clutter so growth, service, and real joy can happen.

The "I don't have any spiritual gifts" excuse comes from years of being overlooked. I've seen people discover surprising talents, prayer, organization, generosity, once they're given steady places to try, fail, and try again. They don't have to be amazing. They just need a shot.

Building Forward: Process Over Perfection

Lasting change comes through process, not perfection. Martin Luther and John Wesley modeled this. They paired new believers with mature ones, built questions into meetings, and made setbacks part of the story. Churches grew, not through dynamic leaders, but because ordinary people had a way to move forward.

Accountability is more than calling someone out. It's seeing them, listening, and reminding them what's possible. People show up when they know they'll be missed. Groups thrive when everyone brings something. Gifts get unearthed in small moments. Someone sets up chairs. Another prays. One more stays late to listen. Every act matters.

If this still feels like too much, start small. One weekly meal. Honest prayer. A question like, "What do you sense the Spirit nudging you to try?" Real change comes in stubborn steps, repeated, within a community that refuses to let you drift.

Showing up on purpose changes everything. You skip a few meetings, drag yourself back... and feel relief. Eventually, joy. People who show up, discover gifts, and serve become magnets. Evangelism just becomes life, lived out loud.

Getting Unstuck: Taking Your Place in the Story

Stop waiting for ideal conditions. Practice works. Your group might muddle through. Someone forgets snacks. Prayers get weird. One guy talks too much. It's fine. What matters is what happens next. Do you show up again? Invite someone? Let quiet voices speak?

Don't know your gift? Try something. Mess up? Great. Now you know what doesn't fit. If it works, you just opened a door. Someone else watching might do the same. Already overwhelmed? Share the work. Groups that last trade the baton around.

If your group's stuck, structure helps. It's not a prison. It's the context where real freedom happens. Enough order lets gifts, stories, and courage breathe.

What's left? Step in. Stumble. Trust the process. You'll get embarrassed. You'll get frustrated. You'll also see breakthrough. The only mistake is standing still and hoping for easy.

I've wanted to quit. I've had weeks where nothing worked. But discipleship isn't a solo project. It's not a shot in the dark. With consistency as your new normal, you'll live out a type of faith that actually sticks. Right in the middle of your ordinary mess.

Real growth doesn't need perfection. It needs a plan, a people, and a persistent Spirit who keeps using ordinary people in extraordinary ways.

11

Chapter 10: Discipleship Rhythms: The 90-Day Growth Plan

When I think about a season in my life when my spiritual growth actually stuck, I remember one thing: it never just happened by accident. I can see now that real growth demands a plan. It never showed up from wishful thinking or vague intentions. So let's talk about what it takes to see real, concrete progress, not just for a week, but for a lifetime.

The Myth of Automatic Growth, and Why Most People Stay Stuck

Plenty of people assume they'll mature spiritually just through showing up to church or reading the occasional verse. Nobody coasts their way into genuine spiritual maturity. Research shows it clearly. Only about a third of folks in church even feel like they're being guided in their growth. When I first saw those stats, I felt a mix of relief and challenge. It wasn't just me. If you want to see your faith move from theory to reality, you can't leave it to chance.

Intentionality matters. John Maxwell says it plainly: spiritual growth is always the result of deliberate action. Deliberate action means much more than just a few big, emotional leaps. It's about steady habits, daily rhythms, and actual accountability. That may sound almost too practical... but the nuts and bolts are what move the needle.

The Three Levers That Make Spiritual Progress Tangible

After years of trial, error, and procrastination disguised as "waiting on a sign," I nailed down three key ingredients that drive sustainable growth:

1. Putting intentionality in the driver's seat: replace aimlessness with a plan.
2. Building real accountability: people who won't let you off easy when you slack.
3. Measuring progress in bite-sized, trackable goals: so you don't wake up three months from now realizing you've gone nowhere.

Joining or forming a small group transforms the spiritual equation. I've watched people move from feeling isolated and uncertain to energized and equipped, sometimes within weeks. People in small groups aren't just learning more. They're actually living what they learn, reporting much higher satisfaction and more grit when life hits hard. That's not random. "Join a group" isn't a magic ticket. But when you set clear aims, meet regularly with people who want the same thing, and have someone checking in on you, even briefly, you create a system that's almost impossible to drift away from.

Building Your Own 90-Day Growth Sprint

I want you to walk out of this chapter with a clear game plan, not just good intentions. This 90-day framework is long enough to see real change, but short enough to feel doable. Here's how the rhythm goes:

Step 1: Join or Launch a Group, But Don't Go It Alone

Whether you're plugging into an existing group or pulling together a few people who want in, commit to showing up weekly. Three to eight people is plenty. Meet at someone's living room, over lunch, or online. The "where" matters less than the "when" and "who." Mark it on your calendar. Treat it like you would a doctor's appointment. Nothing casual about it.

Step 2: Choose One Growth Focus and Speak It Out Loud

At your launch meeting, everyone picks one area to laser in on. It could be upping your Bible reading, finally making prayer a daily thing, or serving consistently in your community. The key is clarity. Vague is the enemy. Say your focus out loud to the group, even if it feels awkward. That little moment turns a wish into a commitment.

Step 3: Pair Up With an Accountability Partner, Make It Quick and Frequent

Each person gets paired with a partner. The check-ins should be short, literally one or two minutes. Text, call, send a voice memo, whatever's fastest and easiest. The secret is frequency, not length. You want someone who'll ask: "Did you hit your reading goal?" or "How did you pray today?" And yes, they'll ask even when you're "busy." That may sound awkward. The awkwardness fades. The results stick.

Step 4: Set Specific, Actionable Growth Goals, Templates Make It Simple

Use a template to map out exactly what you'll aim for, how many chapters you'll read each week, what days you'll serve, what time of day you'll pray. The clearer, the better. This is where most people sabotage their own progress. If you say, "I want to pray more," your brain files that as optional. If you say,

"I'll pray for ten minutes after breakfast on Monday, Wednesday, Friday," it registers as a real task.

Step 5: Keep Touch Points Frequent and Low-Pressure

Accountability that feels like a chore fizzles fast. You want quick check-ins, text "done," snap a photo of your Bible and coffee, whatever works. Consistency is more critical than perfection. Miss a day? Get right back at it. Small nudges compound. Shame doesn't.

Step 6: Coaches and Leaders, the Encouragers and Troubleshooters

If you're leading the group, resist the urge to play warden. Your job is to watch for drift and offer gentle reminders. A quick "Hey, I noticed we're quieter this week, anyone need a boost?" often opens the door for someone to admit they're struggling. When time pressure or disruption hits, brainstorm as a group. Share what's working for others. Often the best solutions come from unexpected places.

Step 7: Pray Like You Mean It, Not Just for Yourself, But for Each Other

Schedule times to pray as a group, even if it's just five minutes at the end of your meeting. Make it less about performance and more about inviting a sense of unity. I've seen walls break down and new energy rise up when people move from "let's get through the agenda" to "let's bring this to God together." It matters. Don't skip this part.

Step 8: End With Celebration, Testimony Night Changes Everything

After 90 days, don't just drift into the next cycle. Mark the finish line. Host a Testimony Night where each person shares one area where they saw God move and how the accountability mattered. It's powerful to hear someone say, "I never finished a reading plan before, but this time I did, and it's because you wouldn't let me quit." Even people who didn't hit every goal feel the momentum. That's when you invite people to take it further, co-lead the next round, or mentor someone else, multiplying the impact.

Why This Works, The Science and the Secret Sauce

The data is clear. Being intentional, setting specific goals and following up, takes you out of autopilot. It breaks the cycle of passivity. The built-in accountability feeds real progress. You want to keep going because you know someone will notice if you disappear. Satisfaction and resilience increase because you're not doing this alone.

This sounds like work. That's the point, it is. But it's the kind of work that pays you back in ways you'll notice fast. You get structure when life is chaotic, support when you feel stuck, and a hunger for the next step that doesn't fade as quickly as last week's inspiration.

Troubleshooting: When Life Happens (Because It Will)

Not every week will go as planned. Schedules explode. Motivation dips. The only thing that kills progress is pretending you're the only one struggling. The group exists to share hacks, not just wins, but workarounds. Maybe that means switching up your meeting time, or picking a new partner if someone flakes out. The people who find ways to keep moving, no matter how small the steps, are the ones still growing months down the road.

If you think accountability is overkill, you might be scared it will actually work. If you're not ready to change, you'll find a dozen reasons to bow out. This plan gives you nothing to hide behind. And that's a good thing.

What Real Progress Looks Like

You'll know this plan is working when the group starts asking bigger questions. Not just "Did you finish?" but "How did it make you feel? What shifted in your life?" People start taking risks, leading prayer, sharing stories, inviting neighbors. The group shifts from "just another meeting" to a launchpad for real growth, spiritually and in every other area of life. This is not a magic bullet. But if you want a track record you can point to, this is your starting line.

Your Turn, Don't Overthink, Just Start

If you're reading this and thinking, "Should I really do this?" pick up your phone and invite someone right now. There's never a perfect moment. The only mistake is putting it off until you feel ready. That day never comes. The first step is the hardest, and it's usually the one nobody regrets.

Getting intentional breaks you out of rut mode. Group accountability turns sporadic effort into a steady climb. The real rewards aren't in flawless performance. They're in sticking with it and seeing what you didn't think possible. If you fall off track? Reach out, show up, and try again. Progress beats perfection every single time.

You now have a blueprint for a 90-day spiritual growth sprint that actually works. Use the templates. Pair up. Make it public, make it personal, and whatever you do, don't try to go alone. This rhythm has changed lives, mine included. No magic. Just action. And that's enough to open up a whole new chapter.

12

Chapter 11: Holy Spirit Activation: Prophetic and Spiritual Gifts in Practice

Life gets predictable when you always rely on your own skills. Real surprise shows up when you invite the Holy Spirit to shake things up. That's not just spiritual talk, it's the best way I know to help people experience something outside the rut of routine. If you've ever wondered how ordinary folks can show up for others in a way that genuinely matters, you're about to learn a process that's simple, a little risky, often awkward, and totally worth it.

Finding the Reason These Gifts Matter

Activating spiritual gifts is not about making anyone look impressive. In fact, it's the opposite. Like Charles Stanley said, "Spiritual gifts are not given to make you spectacular, but to make you a servant." If you want a group that builds people up, encourages, and does it without posturing, you're not alone. Many crave that, but few know where to start.

History backs this up. Look at the Azusa Street Revival or what happened in the book of Acts. People didn't just talk about gifts. They activated them in daily life, and it left a mark that lasted long after the initial excitement. These experiences were practical, simple, and messy in the best way.

The Step-By-Step Listening Prayer

Here is the process. Not a magic formula. A real sequence to apply without feeling fake.

Step 1: Ten Minutes of Listening Prayer

Start with everyone seated. Say, "Okay, set your timer for ten minutes. Silence your phone notifications. Get comfortable." Don't share weekly complaints or even compliments. Begin with actual silence. Breathe. Relax your shoulders.

Quietly ask, "Holy Spirit, is there one encouraging word or Scripture you want to give me for someone here today?" Don't force it. No need to conjure images or make something happen. Just listen. Sometimes you get a fragment, a word, mental picture, song line, or verse. Other times, just a nudge. Write down whatever comes. Don't edit yet.

Next, filter. Look at what you wrote. Does it align with biblical truth? Does it offer hope or encouragement? If it's weird, negative, or self-promoting, toss it. This is not about flexing spiritual muscle. It's about loving someone enough to listen for them.

Step 2: Humble Sharing

When time's up, approach the person. Don't announce, "Thus saith the Lord." Say, "Hey, I was praying for you and I sensed this. Take it or leave it." This invites feedback and keeps ego in check.

Step 3: Do It All Over Again, As a Group

Repeat weekly. Use the same time and place if possible. The more you do it, the less pressure people feel to get everything "right." Each session gets less intimidating. Discuss what happened. Was anything clear? Was it fuzzy? Did anyone take a

CHAPTER 11: HOLY SPIRIT ACTIVATION: PROPHETIC AND SPIRITUAL...

risk and end up encouraging someone in an unexpected way?

Creating a Group Culture That Encourages, Not Embarrasses

Someone will get nervous. That's normal. Someone might say, "I'm afraid of getting it wrong," or worry they'll come across as presumptuous. Call it out. Say, "We're practicing, not performing. You're allowed to miss it." Remind everyone of the boundaries: stay within Scripture, no doom predictions, no declarations about secret sins. Encourage honest feedback. Discourage drama.

If someone goes too far, maybe they claim special insight into someone's life, redirect with, "Remember, our role is encouragement, not control. If your word doesn't build up or offer comfort, park it."

If you're leading, your tone shapes everything. Affirm courage when someone takes a risk, even if they're off. Share your process, including misinterpretations. People relate to honest leaders.

Navigating Mistakes, Awkwardness, and 'Risk With Respect'

Groups will not flow perfectly. Someone will blank. Someone else might get anxious and trip over words. Use mistakes as teachable moments. Say, "You tried. That's what counts." Mistakes are learning tools, not failures.

"Risk with respect" means trying without bulldozing. Share your impression, leave space for response, welcome correction. The messiness reminds you: you're not the source. The Holy Spirit is. Your job is to serve.

After practice, reflect. Did anything come through clearly? Did someone hear a word that clicked for the recipient? Celebrate every small win. Talk through unclear moments. This keeps shame out of the process.

Tracking Growth and Real-Life Breakthroughs

Over time, change shows up quietly. People grow bolder. Words land just when they're needed. A Scripture becomes a lifeline. A kind word restores someone's day.

Encourage testing these spiritual muscles outside the group. In safe settings, it's easy. Real stretch comes at work, the store, or around family. If you sense encouragement for someone and it matches Scripture, share it.

Bottom Line: Discovering Gifts, Serving People

Patterns appear over time. Joe always gets images or dreams. Maria receives Scripture. Others offer simple phrases at the right time. Point out these gifts. People often don't recognize their abilities until someone else names them.

If the group sees a pattern in someone's contributions, say it out loud. Recognition builds confidence. This moves everyone from unsure beginners to a group that actively builds up others, in meetings and beyond.

Skipping this practice for a month brings apathy. Encouragement fades. Now try just a few consistent weeks of practicing together. The difference is obvious. More trust. More boldness. More awkward, wonderful moments that actually make group life worth it.

The goal isn't a slick, polished group that shows off. Aim for honest, servant-hearted people who listen for God, act on what they hear, and stay humble. That's when faith becomes real, accessible, even fun.

13

Chapter 12: Living the Mission: The BLESS Evangelism Challenge

The first time I tried to share my faith outside of a church setting, I felt like I'd just agreed to jump off a high-dive. You know that feeling: there's a ramp, there's an idea, but your stomach is busy running the numbers on what could go wrong. When I heard about the BLESS Evangelism Challenge, it clicked because it wasn't about turning into a megaphone or memorizing a script. It's a challenge, but it's doable and grounded in real relationships, not awkward, forced conversations.

Let's get into it, step by step, so you're not just learning about the BLESS Challenge but actually living it. I'll show you how to turn intention into action, and along the way we'll deal with all the "what-ifs" that threaten to steal your momentum.

Why This Challenge Works (And Doesn't Make You Weird)

I didn't want to make my friends feel like projects. I wanted them to know I actually cared about them, the kind of care that isn't dependent on whether they ever want to talk about Jesus. The BLESS approach works because it's built on active listening, service, and mutual respect. Using it doesn't turn you into the "religious person" everyone avoids at the office or the cookout.

Jesus said to "go into all the world." "All the world" starts with the people you see day in, day out. Whether it's your neighbors, your coworkers, your old high school buddy who is great at borrowing tools but terrible at returning them, it's personal. BLESS turns evangelism from a scary performance into a series of small, faithful steps.

Step One: Build Everything on Prayer (But Make It Specific)

If you skip prayer and jump straight to action, you'll burn out fast or run into walls. So I always start with a list. Not a huge list, just three people for the week. I write down their names, even if I don't have any "deep" conversations in mind. Each morning, I commit to pray for them by name. Not "save my friend" in a generic sense, but real prayers about what's happening in their lives: the layoffs, the sick parent, the new baby, the frustration with a college class.

Why three? Focusing on a handful keeps it realistic. I can be consistent, and it's easier to remember actual details. If you're tempted to pray for 50 people at once, cut it back. This is not a numbers contest.

Step Two: Listen Like It's a Superpower

Once you're praying for someone, you start to care about what they're actually going through. That's where you shift from "talker" to listener. At work, I pay attention to what people mention in passing: the frustration over a difficult boss, the excitement about a new hobby, the sigh that says someone just had a long night. Sometimes, I'll ask, "How's your week going?" and then actually listen for more than just a polite answer.

If you're worried about what to say, stop. Your goal isn't to slide an agenda into the conversation. It's to get the full story. People will share a lot if you just stop filling the silence for them.

Silence is less awkward than fake interest.

Step Three: Share a Meal (Or Coffee Counts, Too)

People relax over food or coffee. You don't have to host a dinner party worthy of a magazine. It could be inviting someone to grab lunch from a food truck, having coffee after a shift, or splitting pizza with your neighbor. Any opportunity to sit together, phones down, is a win.

Don't overthink the menu. The point is presence, not presentation. I once sat in a greasy spoon with a friend after church, and that hour did more for our relationship than months of occasional, polite chit-chat. When you invite people into your ordinary, something shifts. Conversations get real. If you're nervous, confess that you're trying to get better at being present for people in your life. That usually disarms them and opens them up.

Step Four: Serve One Practical Need

I'm not running a charity out of my driveway, but I can mow a lawn for a neighbor after surgery, help a coworker move a couch, or offer to drop off groceries when someone's stuck at home. These small acts build trust. Serving with no strings attached is what makes this stand out. People notice when kindness doesn't come with an ask.

One time, a woman in our group helped an elderly neighbor fix a broken porch light. She didn't leave a tract. She just fixed the light. That relationship grew over months, and eventually, the neighbor started asking questions about why she cared. That's how serving opens up doors naturally.

Step Five: Share Your Story When the Door Opens (Not Before)

People want to know what makes you tick, but only if you're not weird about it. When someone finally asks, "So, why do you care?" or shares a spiritual frustration, respond confidently. This is the moment you've been preparing for.

Keep your story clear and brief. This is not the time for a thirty-minute monologue starting with birth. Hit three points: what your life was like before faith, what changed, and what's different now. Authenticity over polish. If you ramble, they'll remember the rambling, not the point.

If you're sharing the basics of the gospel, keep it simple. Use language they understand, and tie it into the relationship you've already established.

Making the Challenge Stick in a Group

Doing BLESS is easier when you've got others to cheer you on and troubleshoot with you. Each week, our group spends a little time sharing where we're at with the challenge: who we prayed for, what step we're stuck on, and what surprised us. We don't count how many "conversions" happened. That's not up to us. We celebrate progress: "I invited my neighbor to lunch, and he actually said yes!" or, "I got to serve someone and didn't expect anything back."

If someone's hitting a wall, maybe a friend rejected their invitation, we talk through it. Sometimes you just need a brainstorm session: "What could be a low-pressure way to invite them again?" or "How can I listen better instead of worrying about what to say next?" We always finish by praying for the people on our lists. It keeps everyone honest and focused.

Patience, Presence, and When Nothing Seems to Happen

You might do everything "right" and nothing dramatic happens. That's normal. Evangelism isn't a drive-thru. It's the slow work of showing up, again and again, when it would be easier to give up. My friend once spent six months serving one neighbor before they ever opened up about anything meaningful.

That's how trust grows: slow, mostly invisible, but real.

If you're someone who likes instant results, this part will stretch you. Celebrate the small stuff: the new conversation, the first honest answer, the simple "thanks" after a favor. Keep showing up. The win is being there when life falls apart, and you're the only person steady enough to stick around.

Training for the "Now What?" Moment

Eventually, someone will show curiosity about your faith, or open the door. This might happen in the middle of a crisis, or just out of the blue. Be ready to share your story with clarity and humility. Practice a simple, three-minute version with a friend or group member if you need to. Ask for feedback. Does it sound genuine? Is it so full of insider words that no outsider could follow? Be clear, not clever.

If they want to know more about what you believe, have a short way to outline the basics. For example: "God made us to know Him, but we got separated from Him by our own choices. Jesus came to heal that gap. That changed my life." Use your words, not mine. Just don't make it complicated.

Why This Challenge Isn't Optional

Maybe you think you're not ready or that someone else is more qualified. The Great Commission isn't a research project. It's direct orders. Hudson Taylor said, "The Great Commission is not an option to be considered; it is a command to be obeyed."

You're not alone. According to Lifeway, less than half of regular church folk share their faith even occasionally. On the flip side, training makes a difference. Pew found that equipping people increased witnessing by 80 percent. This isn't a contest. This is an invitation to trust that showing up, listening, and serving works, even if it doesn't feel dramatic at first.

Small Steps, Big Multiplications: Experience It for Yourself

Relational evangelism using BLESS isn't just a trendy method. It's a way to multiply your influence without burning out or alienating your network. Every act of service, every story told, every meal shared becomes a seed planted. Some grow fast, some take years, but each one matters. Serving and listening with no expectations stands out. This is how one faithful presence grows into real fruit.

What now? Pick your three. Start praying. Listen harder this week. Invite someone for lunch or coffee. Look for a way to quietly serve. Don't worry about the perfect opening. If that moment comes, be ready with your story, but don't force it. Living the mission happens one BLESS step at a time. Practicing that puts you ahead of the curve.

14

Chapter 13: Building Real Community That Lasts

Nobody warns you how easy it is for a small group to stall out. I've watched folks gather, full of hope, only for things to get awkward, spotty, or downright stale after a few weeks. I've also seen people try to shove themselves into "nice" Christian boxes, hiding how lost they feel, about gifts, about sharing faith, about the whole messy thing. If any part of you dreads your next group meeting, or you've thought, "Maybe this isn't for me," you're not alone. Let's crack open the ugly, honest side of community and kick those nagging doubts in the teeth. I'll answer the questions I hear most, sometimes out loud, sometimes just from that look in someone's eyes.

Q: What if my group just isn't committed?

A: You know when nobody remembers who's bringing snacks, and suddenly nobody's sure when you actually meet? The struggle is real. Commitment in a group starts to wobble when expectations stay fuzzy. I've watched groups try to "just see what happens," and they drift. If you want your group to stick, grab the awkwardness and drag it into the light. Set clear expectations upfront. Make it specific: "We'll meet Wednesdays at 7, everyone brings something, and we're honest if we'll be late or absent." Then, instead of hoping for a big "breakthrough," celebrate small wins like when everyone actually shows up, or someone opens up about a real struggle. Let someone else take the lead sometimes. There are at least two people in your group quietly waiting to step up if given the chance. Rotate who plans, who picks the focus, who hosts. That builds rhythm. It doesn't all land on one person, so nobody flames out.

Just because people scatter for summer or disappear during finals doesn't mean it's game over. If the vibe is off, mention it. "Hey, feels like we're not syncing, should we change something?" If commitment really tanks and nobody cares, don't beat yourself up. Sometimes the mix really is wrong, and it's time to reboot. Every great group I've seen had at least one season where they nearly gave up. Keep going during the dip.

Q: How do I spot my spiritual gifts if I'm not sure I have any?

A: People think "gifted" means loud extrovert who can quote Romans backwards while making soup for fifty. But there's no such thing as a member of the "giftless" club. Every believer gets at least one. Scripture isn't fuzzy on this. The catch is that gifts don't always show up like superhero powers. Sometimes you notice them because other people point them out. You help out and someone says, "Wow, when you listen I just feel seen." Or you organize a messy project and everyone breathes easier. Feedback matters. It's like breadcrumbs leading you to what you're really carrying. Try taking spiritual gift assessments, there are quizzes online or from your church.

If that feels vague, find someone further along in faith who you trust. Ask, "What do you see in me?" This might surprise you. Sometimes a gift hides under something you take for granted like listening or your knack for helping people feel like they belong. Gifts aren't trophies. They're tools meant for building others up. It's not about standing out. It's about serving well.

Q: What if talking about faith feels fake, pushy, or just plain wrong?

A: Most people flinch at evangelism because they think it means cringeworthy moments or polished speeches. It doesn't have to be that way.

If you want to share faith without steamrolling anyone, drop the idea of "closing the sale." Use the BLESS model. Start by genuinely listening, praying quietly, and then serving and caring. Let conversations happen naturally. No pressure. If Jesus never comes up, that's okay. You served, you listened, you blessed, and you did your job. When you focus on the person instead of the project, faith conversations open up. You don't need the right answer. Sometimes just being present when someone asks hard questions makes all the difference.

Q: My schedule is already packed, aren't small groups just another thing to juggle?

A: At first glance, small groups look like one more thing screaming for time. I used to think, "Why commit to another weekly event?"

Small groups can give you resilience and joy. I used to white-knuckle my faith alone. But when you show up to a group faithfully, say, every Wednesday, you start to build a spiritual backbone. Hebrews 10:24-25 says we need each other to push through the grind, remind us why we believe, and catch us when we fall. Some people cut something else to make room and realize the group feeds parts of them nothing else does. You won't find time for community. You make it. Other stuff starts to feel lighter when you do.

Q: I'm really not sure I have spiritual gifts, or that I could use them in any real way. Isn't that for "special" Christians?

A: Spiritual gifts aren't a ranking system. They're not for spiritual "overachievers." According to 1 Corinthians 12:7, gifts are for everyone, for the common good. If your group is limping, someone's holding back. Your gifts are puzzle pieces nobody else has. The moment you stop comparing and start offering, you'll see how it works. People who say, "I'm not gifted," usually haven't tried or never had someone cheer them on. Give your gift a test drive. Organize snacks, lead prayer, ask questions, take attendance, give encouragement. Watch what lights you up and what connects with others. That's your clue.

Q: Evangelism just makes me anxious. Isn't it manipulative to try and "win" people over?

A: Evangelism doesn't have to be about pressure. The BLESS method helps: show up, listen, serve. Let actions speak first. You're not there to trick anyone. If it feels forced, back off. Authenticity wins. Take it slow. Building trust opens more doors than speeches ever could.

Q: What if my group struggles with accountability, or just loses its rhythm?

A: Groups don't run themselves. Politeness leads to silence, which leads to sputtering. Set real expectations together: "We'll show up for each other, be honest when we mess up, and check in when someone's missing." Don't hope it fixes itself. Say, "Have we lost our groove?" Celebrate small wins. Rotate leadership, switch meeting spots. When the group owns the rhythm, it sticks.

Q: Why do groups fall into the trap of avoiding accountability or spiritual growth?

A: Most of the time, it's fear posing as "easygoing." People avoid accountability to dodge judgment or because they're tired. But discipleship grows best in structured, intentional communities. When everything is casual, it gets wobbly. Groups avoiding hard questions or real life lose members. Structure helps: consistent times, honest check-ins, encouragement. Grace doesn't mean zero expectations. The best groups balance honesty with steady support.

Q: Why do people neglect their gifts, or feel stuck using them?

A: Gifts need practice. They're more like muscles than badges. If you only use them once a year or hide them because "someone else is better," they weaken. I've seen gifted encouragers stay silent, or leaders hide, fearing they're pushy. That's not humility, it deprives others. Let your group know what you want to try. Learn by doing. Service sharpens gifts. You'll see how needed you are.

Q: How can I share my faith without feeling robotic, or like a sellout?

A: Evangelism gets easier with practice, but it works best through real relationships. Don't force it. Serve, listen, just be present. When the chance comes, speak from your experience. Say, "This is why faith matters to me." Drop the script. If you're not ready to talk, wait. If you want to stretch, do the BLESS Challenge: bless someone, start a conversation. It gets less awkward over time.

Q: How do you keep a group from becoming just a social club?

A: Social connection is good. But if all you do is eat chips and talk weather, you're missing it. Groups thrive on balance: fun, honesty, spiritual focus. Ask tougher questions, share struggles, challenge comfort zones. Let people share where they see God or where they're stuck. If focus drifts, say, "Are we challenging each other, or just hanging out?" That realigns things.

Q: What if my group resists evangelism, or avoids serving outside itself?

A: Groups gravitate to safety. Push gently. Plan a service project. Pick someone to pray for together. Don't make it a "big thing." Start small, laugh off mistakes, celebrate attempts. Lead by example. Skeptics often get curious and join. It gets easier with every effort.

Q: I'm still nervous about messing this all up. Isn't it easier to stay solo?

A: Solo faith doesn't last. Everyone needs backup. Community is messy. You'll get let down, and you'll let others down. But if you stick it out, show up, invite others, ask hard questions, you get growth, joy, and resilience. Mistakes glue people together. Every strong group has rough patches. The reward is in not quitting at the first bump.

Q: Does all this "structure" kill authenticity?

A: Good structure frees people to be more honest. You don't waste energy on basics. You know where and when to meet, so you can focus on each other. Structure is the walls of the house. It keeps out the rain, so you can be yourself inside. You don't need a script. Just a skeleton to hang things on.

Q: How do I find a mentor for gifts or group leadership?

A: Look for someone you respect who lives what they teach. Say, "Can I pick your brain about leading or using my gifts?" Most people love being asked. If nobody in your group fits, ask at church, or reach out online. Take what helps, leave what doesn't.

Q: If I'm still not "feeling it" in group life or faith growth,

is that a sign to quit?

A: There are dry spells in every faith journey. Sometimes group life feels forced. That's normal. Don't quit. Change one thing: shift the meeting rhythm, invite someone new, change formats, or rest. Nearly every deep group hit a season like that. They kept going. The spark returns.

Q: Any fast hacks for reviving a sleepy group?

A: Swap who leads. Meet somewhere new. Share a meal. Try different formats. Focus on prayer. Serve together. Ask, "What's one thing we wish we did but don't?" Even changing snacks helps. Good pizza or surprise dessert can do wonders.

Small groups work best when you move past autopilot. Structure, purpose, and effort matter. Your gifts matter even when you feel unsure. Evangelism flows naturally when you stop chasing perfect words and start serving with open hands. Mistakes will happen. That's what glues people together.

If your group flopped last semester, or you're leading for the first time and feeling overwhelmed, don't give up. Try again. Tweak something. Ask hard questions. Let grace carry the weight. That group you used to dread might become the people you can't imagine doing faith without.

15

Chapter 14: Recap of Growth and Practice

Let's get straight to the point, this is where I look back on what you've worked through lately and actually spell out what's changed, what you can now reach for, and how you'll recognize progress. You didn't just read random ideas. This last stretch put real, repeatable actions in your hands, stuff you can do alone or with others. If you're still here, you haven't just collected more concepts for your mental shelves. You've started seeing how these pieces fit together and why they matter.

From Foundations to Fruit... What Actually Shifted

If you're thinking, "Did I just get a pile of theory?" no, that's not what happened. What you've just been through is all about practical discipleship, seeing how the Holy Spirit empowers you, and then how that spills out into real-life conversations, relationships, and sometimes messy action. The big headline? This wasn't about passively soaking up info. It was about moving from good intentions to action you can actually track.

So what changed? You've got a structure now for intentional growth. Instead of waiting for spiritual maturity to just happen,

CHAPTER 14: RECAP OF GROWTH AND PRACTICE

you've seen the value of setting clear steps and actually checking back on how it's going. Gone are the days of hoping you'll drift into healthy community or deeper faith. Now, you've got practical handles, stuff that isn't vague or inspirational fluff.

Jumping Into Discipleship That Sticks

Let's talk about the 90-Day Growth Plan. This wasn't just an exercise in planning for planning's sake. Real change rarely sticks without a bit of structure (and probably more reminders than we like to admit). Here, you learned to break down your spiritual goals into bite-sized actions: join or launch a small group, show up weekly (even when you're not feeling it), and actually ask for accountability, meaning you've got someone who'll notice if you've disappeared.

The accountability partner part is the game-changer most people skip. Maybe you've dodged that in the past because it sounded awkward or forced. But when push comes to shove, sporadic check-ins don't really work. Quick encouragements, little nudges, and "Hey, I see you" texts carry more power than most realize. Pair that with customizable templates for prayer, Bible reading, and service? Suddenly, you're not left guessing how to start.

During that launch meeting, if you took it seriously, it probably got a little real. Naming one growth focus out loud in front of others turns intention into something solid. Even if you felt awkward, saying it gives others permission to do the same. That's how group momentum happens.

What Keeps People Stuck (and How You Pushed Past It)

Most folks hit problems like inconsistent attendance, vague goals, or forgetting why they joined. By making regular contact non-negotiable, you outwit the drift toward busy-ness and isolation. Coaches stepped in as gentle prodders. Not taskmasters, but more like "hey, you're still with us, let's keep at it." Milestones, small as they might seem, got celebrated. That's not just about feeling good... it's positive reinforcement in its simplest (and oldest) form.

Where groups usually break down is in skipping accountability or letting rhythms slip. It's easy to rationalize. Life is busy, everyone's got stuff going on. But the fix wasn't rocket science: identify blockages (like time pressure or unclear next steps), brainstorm workarounds, and keep unity and breakthrough a regular prayer topic. Simple doesn't always mean easy, but it does mean doable.

Celebrating Growth... Individually and Together

If you've come this far, you've probably noticed: personal reflection isn't optional. After the 90-day cycle, the group didn't just move on. You gathered up, shared what actually changed, and gave testimony on what accountability brought to the table. It wasn't always a fireworks show of instant maturity, but everyone shared something. That willingness to reflect (even if you were nervous or unsure) brought a new layer of honesty into the group.

Hosting a Testimony Night kind of feels like a big deal, right? Hearing others talk about their own growth (failures and all) creates a sense of shared journey. The group moves from "people I meet with" to actual partners in real change. Some of you even stepped up to co-lead the next round, or at least started thinking about it. That's how multiplication happens. It's not a program. It's growth that's got legs.

Letting the Holy Spirit Lead... In Practice, Not Theory

Some readers maybe felt out of their depth with the "Holy Spirit Activation" bit. That's expected. If you've never tried listening prayer or stepped into sharing encouraging words, you probably felt nervous. But you didn't have to be perfect. The approach was simple: set aside ten minutes, get quiet (harder than it sounds), ask for an encouraging word or Scripture for someone in the group, and write down whatever surfaced.

You filtered impressions through Scripture. Nobody was left guessing whether their idea was out in left field. Sharing with humility (not acting like the oracle of all wisdom) made it safer for everyone. The emphasis? Encourage, don't overstate. That's where most prophetic practice goes off the rails.

Practicing in a group each week did something strange. It made mistakes less scary. You saw that being wrong isn't fatal. Checking what was clear and what was fuzzy together kept things grounded. Leaders modeled this too: gentle corrections, encouragement of "risk with respect," and reminders that every attempt is a learning opportunity.

When stories started surfacing, where a timely word made a real difference, or someone felt genuinely seen, you realized: this isn't a sideshow. It's the building blocks of genuine community. Over time (even if you rolled your eyes at first), you started to spot what spiritual gifts looked like in action, not just in theory. That's another layer of empowerment. Once you can see your gifts at work, it's much easier to take them outside the group.

Evangelism That's Actually Doable (and Not Cringe)

If you've ever backed away from "evangelism" because it sounded like a telemarketing script, you weren't alone. That's why the BLESS Challenge mattered so much. Nobody was strong-arming strangers on the street. The core idea? Pray for three specific people every day, listen to their stories, grab a coffee or meal, meet a practical need, and when the time is right, share your own story.

Role-playing in the group probably felt a bit silly, but it worked the muscle. The more you tried on these scenarios, the less afraid you got of messing up. Reporting back each week wasn't about performing. It was about learning in public. If you got stuck, the group brainstormed what to try next. You celebrated every little breakthrough. Maybe someone asked a good question, or maybe you just made it through a whole conversation without changing the subject.

The best part? No "closing the deal" pressure. It's all about being present and serving with sincerity, not chasing conversions. When someone finally showed spiritual openness, you didn't freeze. You had a simple way to share your story and a way to present the gospel that didn't sound like a sales pitch. Big result? You got a taste of influence that's rooted in honesty and relationship, not bravado or awkwardness.

The Real Bottom Line... You've Got Next Steps

Nothing in the last chapters promises you instant spiritual giant status. That's not what growth is. You've seen that real progress usually looks like slow, awkward starts, little tweaks, and encouragement in the middle of failures. But now, you're not left in the dark. You've got tools to build ongoing growth, confidence to use your gifts, and a way to see evangelism as something organic rather than forced.

The habits you started, regular accountability, practical group practice, serving and listening in the everyday, aren't magic formulas. But they do add up. You've built some momentum. If you stick with it, progress doesn't just fizzle, it compounds. (But hey, nobody will chase you if you don't; ownership is on you.)

You haven't gotten all the answers. But you've got enough to try, fail, adjust, and keep moving. And that's how real change operates: messy, gradual, but absolutely possible.

16

Chapter 15: Keep Building; The Journey Isn't Over

You've made it. Six weeks of wrestling, showing up, praying when it didn't feel easy, and letting God do quiet work under the surface that most people will never see. Maybe you don't feel like you've "arrived." That's okay. This isn't about arrival; it's about foundation.

The goal was never perfection. It was strength that lasts.

Foundations aren't finish lines; they're starting points.

You've laid down something real, and now we get to keep building together. I've walked these same steps, still do most days. There are mornings I have to remind myself of what's already true, and evenings when I still go back to the same Scriptures that steadied me years ago. The work never stops; it just deepens.

Faith Was Never Meant to Stop at the Ground Floor

Every story in Scripture starts small, a whisper, a seed, a yes nobody notices at first. God doesn't hand out blueprints for skyscrapers until He sees that we're serious about pouring the slab.

That's what these six weeks have been about, digging deep, setting what's unseen, and trusting that what's below the surface will hold what's yet to come.

Now it's time to live from that foundation.

"Starter faith" was never meant to stay small. It's meant to stretch, to reach, to risk. Foundations exist so that growth can happen without collapse. That means we don't stop here; this is where real life begins.

The Real Test Starts Now

There's no Week Seven checklist waiting. No more pages telling you what to do next. Just life, real, unpredictable, beautiful, and complicated life.

That's the point.

The rhythm we've built, prayer, Scripture, accountability, obedience, is the scaffolding that holds us steady when everything else shifts. Don't underestimate the small things. They're what keep the structure sound when feelings fade or pressure rises.

When you start to drift, return to what's simple. Open your Bible. Pray again. Reach out again. Repent again. Obey again. God meets us in the return, ready to rebuild, not with disappointment, but with fresh strength. I've had to do that countless times, finding grace waiting every single time. That's how I know it works.

Growth That Outlasts Us

The next stretch of this journey isn't just about you or me. Real faith multiplies; it spills over into the lives around us.

Someone nearby needs what you've just walked through.

Someone's waiting for your story, your scars, your quiet endurance. Don't wait to feel qualified. Invite someone to coffee, open your Bible, share what you've learned. That's discipleship in motion, ordinary people passing on a steady faith to others.

That's how the Kingdom grows, not through spotlight moments, but through people who decide they're not giving up. I've watched it happen again and again, faith passed on through small, faithful moments that no one sees until years later when fruit starts to show.

A Word About Finishing Well

Faith isn't a sprint; it's a lifetime of construction. There will be cracks, leaks, slow seasons, and times when you wonder if anything is changing. But stillness isn't failure. Roots grow down before fruit grows up.

Keep showing up. Keep letting God dig deeper. The unseen work is what makes the visible fruit last. I know what it's like to think you're stuck when God's actually building strength underneath. That realization has saved me more than once.

Your Next Steps

If you're asking, "What now?" here's where we go from here:

1. **Keep the habits.** The small ones matter. They aren't routines; they're reinforcements.
2. **Stay in rhythm.** Stay connected. Join a group or start one. Growth withers in isolation but multiplies in community.
3. **Walk with someone new.** Mentor, listen, or guide. You don't need to be perfect to lead; you just need to stay honest.
4. **Begin the 90-Day Growth Plan.** Give God three more

CHAPTER 15: KEEP BUILDING; THE JOURNEY ISN'T OVER

months of consistent obedience and watch what He builds.
5. **Stay teachable.** Never assume you've mastered the basics. They're the anchors that hold when storms return.

A Final Word

You might have started this journey uncertain, tired, or searching for something solid again. But look at what's been built, something living, rooted, and ready to grow.

This isn't the end. It's the foundation for everything that comes next.

And we're still here, still building, still believing, still walking this out beside you. I'm still learning right alongside you, discovering that God's patience outlasts every rough patch we walk through.

"And I am sure of this, that He who began a good work in you will bring it to completion at the day of Jesus Christ."

— *Philippians 1:6 (ESV)*

Keep going. Keep building. The story isn't finished, and the foundation you've laid is only the beginning.

Now that we've come to the final chapter of this journey, if you're ready to keep building and want to go deeper into understanding who you are in Christ, consider reading my companion book, *Called by Name: Unlock the Unshakeable Identity God Already Spoke Over You*. It's designed to help you solidify your identity and walk in the confidence of who God says you are. It's the natural next step after this manual, where *Starter Faith* builds your foundation, *Called by Name* helps you discover who stands on it. You can find it now on Amazon.

Appendix A: The Foundation Builder's Toolkit

Purpose: Knowledge fades; habits stick. This toolkit turns the six weeks into repeatable practices and public steps that hold when storms hit.

How to Use This Toolkit

- Keep this toolkit open during Weeks 5–6 and for the 30 days after you finish.
- Do one small action each day; don't go two days in a row without using it.
- Use a pen-sign, date, and check boxes.
- Pair up-share progress with your accountability partner.
- Revisit the **Foundations Audit** each week to pick your next step.

APPENDIX A: THE FOUNDATION BUILDER'S TOOLKIT

1) Statement of Salvation (Write it. Sign it. Speak it.)

How to use: Write it once, read it aloud daily for 7 days, then weekly; store it in your Bible and save a photo on your phone.
What to do:

- Use the template, fill in your own words, sign and date it.
- Read it aloud daily for 7 days, then weekly for a month.

Why it works: It anchors identity in truth over emotion and ends the "am I really in?" cycle.
Template

- **What Jesus did for me:** _____
  _____
- **My response (confessed and believed):** _____
  _____
- **Who I am now (in Christ):** _____
  _____

Signed: _____ Date: _____ / _____ /
_____

7-**Day Reading Log:** M T W T F S S (initial each day)

2) Baptism: 30-Day Obedience Plan

How to use: Set a baptism date within 30 days, complete one step this week, and text your plan to two witnesses. **Commitment:** "I will be baptized within the next 30 days."
Target Date: _____ / _____ / _____

Steps this week:

1. Contact church / leader: _____ (by //___).
2. Invite at least two witnesses: _____ and _____.
3. Share your Statement of Salvation with them before your baptism.

Why now: Delay feeds doubt; public obedience builds traction.

3) Daily Prayer Pattern (10 Minutes)

How to use: Take 10 minutes each morning; set a phone reminder and keep names/needs on one list.

- **Adore (2 min):** Who God is today.
- **Align (3 min):** "Your kingdom come..." today's schedule & decisions.
- **Ask (3 min):** Specific names & needs.
- **Act (2 min):** One obedience you'll do before noon.

Tip: Keep it simple and consistent. Prayerless days become powerless days.

4) Accountability Covenant (Lightweight & Real)

How to use: Choose a partner, lock a 15-minute weekly slot, and keep it even when it's awkward. **Partner(s):** _____ | **Check-in day/time:** _____

We agree to:

- Ask 2 honest questions each week: *Where did you obey? Where did you hide?*
- Name 1 action by next check-in (SMART).
- Pray out loud for 60 seconds each.

If a check-in is missed: reschedule within 48 hours.
Lone rangers are easy prey-build guardrails, not guilt.

5) Evangelism Prompt Cards (Speak, don't just signal)

Cut these out or copy them to your phone-use one prompt this week.

- "This might sound simple, but Jesus changed _____ in my life. Can I tell you in one minute?"
- "I'm taking a fresh step with God. Is there anything I can pray about for you right now?"
- "I wrote a one-paragraph 'why I follow Jesus.' Would you give me feedback?"

A silent witness becomes a slothful witness-practice going public in love.

6) Gifts & Serving: From Spectator to Servant (Mini-Activation)

How to use: Circle two gifts you'll lean into and schedule one concrete serving opportunity this month. Circle two you sense fit you now: **Encouragement · Helps · Hospitality · Teaching · Mercy · Administration · Giving · Evangelism · Prayer · Prophetic insight.**

One way I'll serve this month: _____

_____

Who I'll tell (for accountability): _____

_____

Move from watching to working–start small, start now.

7) The Storm Playbook (Rehearse before it hits)

How to use: Pre-choose your anchor passage now; when trouble hits, walk the five steps without debating. When fear, loss, betrayal, or temptation hits, do this sequence:

1. **Declare** your Statement of Salvation aloud (identity first).
2. **Call** your accountability partner; ask for 60 seconds of prayer now.
3. **Open** to your anchor passage (pre-choose one: Romans 8, Psalm 27, John 15).
4. **Act** on one small obedience within one hour (text apology, cancel compromise, schedule hard convo).
5. **Record** what you learned in two sentences.

8) Foundations Audit (Rate 1–5)

How to use: Rate yourself on Sunday night; your lowest score becomes your top action for the week.

- Clear, speakable salvation story: ___ *(goal: 4–5)*
- Baptism scheduled/completed: ___ *(goal: 5)*
- Daily prayer pattern consistency: ___ *(goal: 4–5)*
- Weekly accountability: ___ *(goal: 4–5)*
- Active service using a gift: ___ *(goal: 4–5)*
- Verbal witness this month: ___ *(goal: 4–5)*

Your lowest score = your next step this week.

9) Commissioning & Benediction (Speak this over yourself or your group)

How to use: Speak this out loud at the end of Week 6 and again after your baptism. "Father, thank You for establishing me on the foundation of Jesus. I renounce delay, passivity, and fear. I choose public obedience, daily prayer, honest accountability, and courageous witness. Make my life a shelter for many. In Jesus' name, amen."

Appendix B: Lead Someone to Salvation (Simple Conversation Guide)

How to use: Keep this on your phone or a card. When God opens a door, stay loving and clear. Ask, listen, and invite.

The 5-Step Flow

1. **Care & Pray (30 seconds):** Be present. Ask a real question about their life; pray silently for clarity and courage.
2. **Share Your 1-Minute Story:** *Before – Jesus – After.* (Keep it concrete.)
3. **Explain the Gospel in 4 Words:**

- **God:** Holy and loving; made us for Himself (Genesis 1; John 3:16).
- **Us:** We've sinned and can't fix ourselves (Romans 3:23).
- **Jesus:** Lived, died, and rose to save us (1 Corinthians 15:3–4).
- **Response:** Turn to Him and trust Him (Acts 3:19; Romans 10:9–10; Ephesians 2:8–9).

1. **Ask the Question:** "Do you believe this and want to follow Jesus today?"

- If **yes:** move to the prayer below.
- If **not yet:** honor their pace; offer to keep walking with them.

1. **Pray & Confess (out loud):** Invite them to pray in their own words. You can guide:

"Jesus, I believe You died for my sins and rose again. I turn from my sin and trust You to save me. Be my Lord. I give You my life. Amen."

Immediate Next Steps (if they decide)

- **Assurance:** Read Romans 10:9–10 and 1 John 5:11–13 together.
- **Tell someone today:** their friend/family or your accountability partner.
- **Baptism:** Set a date within 30 days (use the plan in Section 2).
- **First steps:** Start the Daily Prayer Pattern and read the Gospel of Mark; meet weekly for 4 weeks.

Do's & Don'ts

- **Do** keep Jesus central; **don't** get lost in debates.
- **Do** use Scripture; **don't** pressure or manipulate.
- **Do** ask clear questions; **don't** rely on perfect answers.
- **Do** invite a response; **don't** make a formula the focus-faith is in Christ, not in wording.

Common Roadblocks (with gentle replies)

- **"I'm not good enough."** - None of us are; that's why Jesus came (Ephesians 2:8–9).
- **"I've done too much wrong."** - His grace is greater (1 Timothy 1:15–16).
- **"I still have questions."** - Faith begins with the light you have; we'll keep learning together (Mark 9:24).

Appendix C: Scripture Declarations & Memory Cards

How to use: Keep these Scriptures visible - on your phone lock screen, mirror, or desk. Each item includes a verse, a short declaration, and a simple next action. Copy the card template at the end to make your own.

Identity in Christ

1. **2 Corinthians 5:17** - "If anyone is in Christ, he is a new creation…"

   - **Declaration:** In Jesus, I am made new today.
   - **Action:** Tell your accountability partner one way you will live as new.

1. **Romans 8:1** - "There is therefore now no condemnation…"

   - **Declaration:** Condemnation is not my judge - the Spirit leads me.
   - **Action:** When guilt rises, speak this verse out loud once in the morning and once at night.

1. **Galatians 2:20**

- **Declaration:** Christ lives in me – I live by faith in Him.
- **Action:** Start your day with "Jesus, live through me today."

Assurance & Salvation

1. **Romans 10:9-10**

- **Declaration:** I have confessed and believe – I am saved.
- **Action:** Read your Statement of Salvation out loud.

1. **1 John 5:11-13**

- **Declaration:** God gave me eternal life – I know that I have it in the Son.
- **Action:** Write this passage on a card and carry it for a week.

Obedience & Baptism

1. **Acts 2:38**

- **Declaration:** I respond to Jesus with public obedience.
- **Action:** If not baptized, set your target date today (Appendix A, Section 2).

1. **John 14:15**

- **Declaration:** I love Jesus – so I choose to obey Him.
- **Action:** Name one command you will practice today.

Prayer & Dependence

1. **Philippians 4:6-7**

- **Declaration:** I choose prayer over anxiety - God's peace guards me.
- **Action:** Use the Daily Prayer Pattern from Appendix A.

1. **Luke 11:9-13**

- **Declaration:** The Father gives the Holy Spirit to those who ask.
- **Action:** Ask boldly for the Spirit's help with one decision.

Witness & Courage

1. **Acts 1:8**

- **Declaration:** I am a witness - the Spirit empowers me.
- **Action:** Use one Evangelism Prompt this week (Appendix A, Section 5).

1. **Romans 1:16**

- **Declaration:** I am not ashamed of the gospel.
- **Action:** Share your 1-minute story with one person.

Perseverance in Trials

1. **James 1:2-4**

- **Declaration:** Trials grow me toward maturity.
- **Action:** Name one Christ-like response you will practice in today's pressure.

1. **Psalm 27:13-14**

- **Declaration:** I will see the goodness of the Lord - I wait with courage.
- **Action:** Add this to your Storm Playbook (Appendix A, Section 7).

Appendix D: Foundations FAQ and Troubleshooting Guide

How to use: When you hit a snag, find the matching scenario, read the truth, then take the one next action. Keep it simple. No printouts needed.

1) "Some days I still doubt my salvation."

What might be happening: Feelings are shifting and you are still learning to trust God's promise. **Truth:** Romans 10:9-10, 1 John 5:11-13. God saves by grace through faith, not by perfect feelings. **One next action:** Read your Statement of Salvation out loud and text your partner that you did it. See Appendix A, Section 1. **10-second prayer:** "Jesus, I trust Your finished work more than my feelings." **Red flag:** If condemnation and fear are constant for weeks, tell a pastor for care.

2) "I keep delaying baptism."

What might be happening: Perfectionism or fear of going public. **Truth:** Acts 2:38, Acts 8:36-38. Obedience is the point, not performance. **One next action:** Set a date on your calendar today. See Appendix A, Section 2. **10-second prayer:** "Lord, I choose obedience today. Give me boldness." **Red flag:** If delays continue after setting a date, invite a friend to hold you to it.

3) "Prayer feels dry or scattered."

What might be happening: You're trying to do too much or keep it vague. **Truth:** Matthew 6:6, Philippians 4:6-7. Simple, honest prayer matters. **One next action:** Use the 10-minute pattern tomorrow morning. See Appendix A, Section 3. **10-second prayer:** "Father, meet me as I come simply." **Red flag:** Persistent numbness with heavy sadness may signal you need pastoral and professional support.

4) "I fell back into an old sin."

What might be happening: Hiddenness and isolation weaken resolve. **Truth:** 1 John 1:9, Proverbs 28:13. Confession and light restore traction. **One next action:** Call your partner and confess today. Make one change to remove the trigger. **10-second prayer:** "Jesus, thank You for cleansing and power to walk clean." **Red flag:** If the pattern is addictive, ask a leader for a recovery group referral.

5) "I feel spiritual pushback or fear at night."

What might be happening: Normal resistance as you grow. **Truth:** Ephesians 6:10-18, Psalm 4:8. You have armor and authority in Christ. **One next action:** Read Psalm 27 or Romans 8 out loud and pray with your partner. See Appendix A, Section 7. **10-second prayer:** "In Jesus' name I stand firm in peace." **Red flag:** If fear includes panic or self-harm thoughts, seek immediate pastoral and professional help.

APPENDIX D: FOUNDATIONS FAQ AND TROUBLESHOOTING GUIDE

6) "I was hurt by church before and feel wary."

What might be happening: Protective walls from past pain. **Truth:** Hebrews 10:24-25, Romans 12:5. We heal in healthy community. **One next action:** Try one low-risk step: attend, linger 10 minutes to meet one person, or join a group for 4 weeks. **10-second prayer:** "Lord, guide me to safe, wise relationships." **Red flag:** Abuse or manipulation is never ok. If you see it, step out and inform trusted leaders.

7) "My family or friends push back on my new faith."

What might be happening: Fear of change or misunderstanding. **Truth:** 1 Peter 3:15, Matthew 5:16. Gentle witness speaks loudly. **One next action:** Share your 1-minute story and ask how you can serve them this week. **10-second prayer:** "Jesus, make me both clear and kind." **Red flag:** If hostility becomes threatening, set boundaries and seek help from leaders.

8) "I feel unqualified to share my faith."

What might be happening: Comparison and fear of not knowing enough. **Truth:** Acts 1:8, John 9:25. A simple story and the Spirit are enough. **One next action:** Use Appendix B's 5-step flow with one open friend. **10-second prayer:** "Holy Spirit, empower my words and love." **Red flag:** None. Start small.

9) "I am overwhelmed by schedule and can't keep progress."

What might be happening: No clear priority or small steps. **Truth:** Matthew 6:33, Ephesians 5:15-16. Seek first and make the best use of time. **One next action:** Pick one action from Appendix A for today only. Schedule tomorrow's 10 minutes before bed. **10-second prayer:** "Lord, order my day around You." **Red flag:** If you never rest, plan a weekly Sabbath block and tell your partner.

10) "How do I know if God is speaking or if it's just me?"

What might be happening: Learning to test and confirm. **Truth:** John 10:27, 1 Thessalonians 5:19-21, James 3:17. His wisdom is pure, peaceable, and aligns with Scripture. **One next action:** Write what you sense, test it by Scripture, seek wise counsel, and look for peace. **10-second prayer:** "Speak Lord, your servant is listening." **Red flag:** If impressions lead to secrecy, shame, or control, reject them and ask for counsel.

Quick Index

- Assurance – see 1 and Appendix C
- Baptism – see 2 and Appendix A
- Prayer – see 3 and Appendix A
- Temptation – see 4 and Appendix A, Section 7
- Spiritual warfare – see 5 and Appendix A, Section 7
- Church wounds – see 6
- Family pushback – see 7

APPENDIX D: FOUNDATIONS FAQ AND TROUBLESHOOTING GUIDE

- Evangelism confidence – see 8 and Appendix B
- Time and priorities – see 9
- Hearing God – see 10

Made in the USA
Coppell, TX
23 November 2025

63765235R00085